Patricia calls mothers, fathers, [barcode: MW00792054]
Christi to guide the younger ge.
wholehearted, abandoned love for Jesus in keeping with becoming the
Bride of Christ and living the first and great commandment.

　　—Mike Bickle, *International House of Prayer*

John and Patricia have been spiritual children of my husband and me for
over twenty-five years. We have watched firsthand how they have raised
their children. They have truly raised ones with burning hearts—loving
Jesus, loving each other, and wanting to impact the next generation.
We highly recommend Patricia's book. It gives practical and extremely
helpful ways to raise your children and mentor them to be fruitful, godly
leaders.

　　—Carol Arnott, *Catch the Fire Toronto*

The younger generation is crying out for mentors: fathers and mothers
who can nurture and give guidance, affirmation, and covering.
Many of these ones have been raised in broken homes with parental
abandonment, and even in the church there is oftentimes little spiritual
or life mentoring. For years, Patricia Bootsma and her husband have
brilliantly and effectively stepped up to the plate.

If anyone could write a book on this subject that would exhort and
impart the heart and the skills for mentoring these ones, it would be
Patricia. I love her passion to see the next generation arise to be all
they can be—to fulfill their God-given destiny in character, calling, and
gifting. Through this book, she will surely encourage you to step into a
glorious grace from your heavenly Father to pour love and nurture into
this generation of precious treasures and reformers.

　　—Patricia King, *XP Ministries*

There is no one I know more qualified to write a book on raising and mentoring next generation lovers of God than Patricia Bootsma. She is one of my heroes. Having raised six kids of her own—homeschooling them while pastoring churches, speaking around the world, building houses of prayer, and launching prophetic roundtables—she has earned the right to speak on this subject. This book is not simply theory—it is filled with the kind of practical wisdom that only comes from having lived out what is being taught. If you could only meet the author and her incredible children, you would not hesitate to put into practice everything this book teaches. I more than highly recommend it.

—Stacey Campbell, *RevivalNOW! Ministries*
Canadian Prophetic Council

In *Raising Burning Hearts*, Patricia Bootsma encourages every parent to take seriously the call to pray for and over their children. She shares testimonies from her heart as a mother and as an intercessor. Patricia takes us along on an honest journey into the power of God to give wisdom and understanding to parents who desire to raise children fully equipped to follow Him. She trusted God even in the tiny things for each child, and you will be blessed and encouraged as she unfolds her experiences in answered prayer. It will build up your faith and inspire you also to pray over each child, everyday and in every season, and to raise them with the wisdom of God.

—Julie Meyer, *International House of Prayer*

I am blessed to endorse Patricia Bootsma's new book, *Raising Burning Hearts: Parenting and Mentoring Next Generation Lovers of God*. Running after intimacy with Jesus and studying scripture should be normal practices for all Christian families. Patricia's conviction that we need to expose our children to the glory and presence of God especially touched my heart. She emphasizes that by guiding parents not to compromise our Christian morals and values, we are truly keeping God's word alive to the next generation. It is refreshing that she models in her own home what she puts to paper.

— Heidi G. Baker, PhD, *Iris Global*

RAISING BURNING HEARTS

RAISING BURNING HEARTS

Parenting and Mentoring Next Generation Lovers of God

PATRICIA BOOTSMA

Foreword by Mike Bickle

FORERUNNER
PUBLISHING
KANSAS CITY, MISSOURI

Raising Burning Hearts
by Patricia Bootsma

Published by Forerunner Publishing
International House of Prayer
3535 E. Red Bridge Road
Kansas City, MO 64137

ihopkc.org/books

Forerunner Publishing is the book-publishing division of the International House of Prayer of Kansas City, an evangelical missions organization that is committed to praying for the release of the fullness of God's power and purpose, as we actively win the lost, heal the sick, feed the poor, make disciples, and impact society.

ISBN: 978-1-938060-18-2

Cover design by Gedy Rivera & Isaac Weisman
Page layout design by Isaac Weisman, Ian Barker & Megan Olander

Printed in the United States of America

I'd like to dedicate this book first of all to my heavenly Father. You have parented me so well. For eternity I will love and worship You.

I dedicate it also to John, my husband of twenty-four years. Besides the Lord Himself, the biggest reason we have six amazing children is your love, your fathering, and the fact that you are a man after God's own heart. I'm really glad I married you!

Lastly, I dedicate this to my children—Judah, Gabrielle, Aquila, Phoebe, Zoe, and Glory Anna—and to our daughter-in-law, Bethany, and grandsons, Josiah and Hasten Justice. Keep being the burning hearts you are. I love you all so much.

CONTENTS

FOREWORD

*For though you might have ten thousand instructors in
Christ, yet you do not have many fathers; for in Christ
Jesus I have begotten you through the gospel. Therefore I
urge you, imitate me.*
1 CORINTHIANS 4:15–16

As FOLLOWERS OF JESUS WE are all called to obey the Great Commission. It is a command to disciple people so that they can feed
themselves in the Word, hear from God for their own lives, make
godly choices, minister to others, and then in turn disciple younger
believers. But what is the most effective way to do this? Talking to
the Corinthians, Paul recognizes that while instruction from teachers is good, it is no substitute for the example of a true spiritual
father.

This is the first generation in which children are influenced
more outside their home than inside it. In fact, we face a crisis
in our day due to the lack of spiritual fathers and mothers in the
home, society, and even in the church. We must face this problem
head on, realizing the magnitude of the challenge ahead. Because
we are called to make disciples, the church must embrace the call to
father and to mother. Mature believers are meant to model the way
for those who follow, both our natural, physical children and also
those individuals whom God has placed in our spiritual families. A
parent's impact far outweighs any other—which is why I appreciate
Patricia Bootsma's message in *Raising Burning Hearts.*

Patricia and her husband, John, not only teach about parenting and mentoring, but they live what they preach. We have been privileged to have had two of their six children attend International House of Prayer University for the past few years and become part of our spiritual family here in Kansas City, and I can say they have been a delight. These young women have displayed integrity and passion for the things of God; they are evidence of the fruit of John and Patricia's approach to parenting.

Patricia brings the indispensable perspective of a mother. There is perhaps no greater responsibility than to disciple the next generation in the ways of the Lord. This is clearly the duty of both parents. And while a pastor or Sunday school teacher may connect with a child for a limited time each week, it is often the mothers who are spending countless hours every day with their little ones—what a responsibility! In my opinion, women have been the largest, most diligent and effective work force in the kingdom throughout history, and mothers are the most successful in making disciples. One of Satan's main strategies has been to minimize the value and effectiveness of motherhood. The Lord is raising up passionate lovers of Jesus who will resist this demonic strategy. Jesus is restoring honor to women in the home, the church, and in workplaces that are built on kingdom principles.

The great need for spiritual fathers and mothers is glaringly evident—and not just to the older generation. I encounter so many young people who deeply desire a spiritual mentor. I often turn their search inside out, encouraging them to set their heart on becoming a spiritual father or mother to younger believers instead of simply seeking to be mentored themselves. As a command to disciple people, the Great Commission is applicable to all believers. Patricia and John's example is not just for the fully mature or physical parents. Discipling someone else is actually the first step to becoming a spiritual leader, and in this process the young person will find that as they stay one step ahead of those they mentor, they too are becoming discipled.

As Paul said, there may be many teachers, but there are few fathers. We should follow his example, becoming true parents and teaching our children (spiritual and physical) to imitate us in obeying Jesus. Patricia and John have done this, and as the church steps up to the need and the call, I believe this book will be a valuable resource, helping to restore the dignity of the responsibility we have as mothers and fathers.

Mike Bickle
October 2014
Kansas City

INTRODUCTION

THIS BOOK IS DESIGNED FOR the parent who longs primarily for their children to excel in what really matters in life—loving God with all of their heart, soul, mind, and strength. Out of the place of an awakened, burning heart we can see them live out the fullness of His destiny for them.

This book is also for those who mentor children, teenagers, and young adults, not necessarily as biological but as spiritual parents. The apostle Paul stated in First Corinthians 4:15, "For though you might have ten thousand instructors in Christ, yet you do not have many fathers; for in Christ Jesus I have begotten you through the gospel." There is a desperate need for spiritual fathers and mothers to help mold a generation to walk in their God-given calling.

Desiring for our children and those in our influence to be doctors, nurses, lawyers, musicians, missionaries, leaders, or politicians is indeed noble. Yet keeping the first commandment in first place and "majoring on the majors" is necessary to instill in them a value for loving and obeying the One who created them for greatness. Out of that place of putting Him and His ways in the center, all the rest is added on as a bonus.

God is raising up generations who wholeheartedly seek Him and love Him with a burning passion. Jesus is indeed coming again to the earth, this time as the Bridegroom King, victorious and glorious. That monumental event is coming soon. It will be preceded by a great ingathering of souls, as many come to know Him. The love of the bride of Christ for the coming Bridegroom will burn brightly—evidenced by worshiping prayer warriors on the earth, helping to usher in His return.

To that end, the purpose of this book is to help raise up generations of burning lovers of God, awakened in truth, advancing in their destiny, and helping to prepare the way for the coming of the Lord.

I've always been burdened with a strong desire to fulfill the God-given destiny on my life, as well as see all in the body of Christ fulfill theirs. I was an eight-year-old farmer's daughter when two strangers visited the family farm and began to speak to me. They said I would be greatly used of God, travel the world preaching, lead many to Jesus, and be involved in a great move of the Spirit. My child's brain couldn't grasp what they were saying, especially since I was raised in a church where there were no women in ministry. However, my heart burned as they spoke those words. I asked my mom, working nearby, who the people talking to me were. She replied that she didn't see anyone speaking to me. I knew what I had seen and heard, and in later years I would read Hebrews 13:2, which speaks of angels who come in human form. Whether they were angels or not, I cannot prove. However, there was something sealed on my heart that day—a burning desire to know God and make Him known.

My husband and I have been a part of the senior leadership team of Catch the Fire Toronto (formerly Toronto Airport Christian Fellowship) since 1995. We have been privileged to be part of a move of the Spirit that has touched millions around the globe. We have seen the Father's love poured out, hearts and bodies healed, souls saved, and the Holy Spirit's powerful touch awakening hearts in intimate love. Since 2003, we have also been part of the worship and prayer movement sweeping the globe. I help lead and build houses of prayer locally and abroad. It has been exciting and rewarding, yet there is a priority that comes before ministering to others, taking the stage, or obtaining titles.

The greatest ministry we will have is the ministry within our own home. As Jesus modeled, our highest priority is to give to those closest to us, those we parent and mentor. I don't want to change the world only to lose my children to it in the process. My ministry begins with ministering to the Lord, then my husband and my children.

I'm not a psychologist, nor a theologian. I don't subscribe to a particular, popular child-rearing strategy. I am a mother of six children, ranging in age from twenty-three to eleven—Judah, Gabrielle, Aquila, Phoebe, Zoe, and Glory Anna—who passionately love the Lord and are walking in ever-increasing levels of their prophetic destiny. I have numerous spiritual children whom I have had the privilege of influencing. I love the Lord; I love His Word and His ways. I write from these real-life experiences, and my hope is to see many more of the next generation released into their destinies. At the end of each chapter you will find testimonials from my children and others, sharing how the principles described impacted their lives and relationships with God.

I certainly haven't done everything right in parenting. I remember many times I have made mistakes or not followed the very advice I am giving. I have at times had nothing to say except, "I'm sorry. Lord, I'm sorry." In those moments, the Lord's voice, in my spirit, has interrupted my self-abasement, "Patricia, I cover your mistakes." His peace sweeps anxiety away. I know that as I do my part in parenting, God will do His part, and He will bring good where I was weak. He is the best Father ever!

Some of you reading this book may think, "Oh, I wish I had known some of these things years ago." Others may not like some of what you read. I'm not one to shy away from what may be deemed controversial, or to adhere to political correctness. What I'm more concerned about is biblical faithfulness and truth. You may not agree with all that is written. Feel free to "spit the pits from the pie," but, by all means, inquire of the Lord yourself for His best child-rearing and mentoring strategies.

A prophetically gifted friend of mine had a dream recently of the worldwide revival the Lord is about to bring to the earth. In the dream the years were fast-forwarded and he was an older man surrounded by young Christian leaders in the greatest revival the world has ever seen. They were asking him, in his old age, how the great awakening had started. "How did the revival start?" they inquired. "We ask because the world is on fire."

In his dream, my friend replied, "It began with the burning ones. Young men and women would gather together in burning rooms, and they began to call out for the fire of God. Houses of prayer and worship were springing up all over the globe, and they were known for their fire. They were known as burning rooms, full of burning ones, crying out day and night for the fire of God to sweep the planet."

He recounts, "I sat back and felt such love for these young leaders. I felt like a proud father. I was amazed at the hunger from these ones, and poured into them everything I could from my years of following the Lord and being able to witness the beginnings of the massive revival the world was in."

A world burning for Jesus begins with His bride's heart burning for Him—that means mothers and fathers and sons and daughters. As a mother in the natural and in the faith, I want to help raise a generation to burn with passion and zeal for the One who is worthy of our abandoned devotion.

It is my prayer that in this book you will find nuggets of wisdom and tools of truth to use as you walk the high calling of parenthood or mentoring. It really is true that the time we have the next generation in our grasp and in our homes goes so fast. Enjoy the journey. Indeed, "Children are a heritage from the Lord, the fruit of the womb is a reward" (Psalm 127:3).

1

BE A MODEL

Imitate me, just as I also imitate Christ.
1 Corinthians 11:1

Thomas is bright, focused, and calculated. His father, a chief executive officer of a company with various industrial plants scattered across North America, is also a man of faith and character who loves his wife and three children deeply. Thomas, now a junior in the University of Notre Dame's business degree program, always has admired his father and is on track to be just like him.

Lindsay has had two driving under the influence (DUI) incidents and three stays in rehabilitation facilities. She has spent some time in jail and is working on fulfilling court-ordered community service projects. Lindsay's father, a former Wall Street trader, is an alcoholic and cocaine user who has spent numerous years in jail on charges such as insider trading, contempt of court, DUI, and domestic dispute. Lindsay despises her father, will not speak with him, and is on track to be just like him.

What is the influence in the lives of Thomas and Lindsay directly linked to where they are today? Parental modeling.

Fred's father abandoned him and his mother when Fred was two years old. This caused Fred many insecurities in his childhood development. When Fred entered middle school, a middle school teacher and high school basketball coach began to spend extra time with Fred, teaching him, training him, and taking him under his proverbial wing. He helped set Fred on a path of achievement and destiny and modeled what a father and husband should look like.

Timothy's mother, Eunice, and grandmother, Lois, were godly women, but his father was an unbelieving Gentile. Paul starts the First Epistle to Timothy stating the following, "Paul, an apostle of Jesus Christ, by the commandment of God our Savior and the Lord Jesus Christ, our hope, to Timothy, a true son in the faith."

What was the influence in Fred and Timothy's lives linked to how their lives were lived? Mentor modeling.

PARENTAL AND MENTOR MODELING

Whether we know it or not, or like it or not, as parents and mentors, the loudest words we speak are the lives we live. Little eyes are watching, little ears are hearing, and family patterns are being propagated.

If we exemplify in our lives and homes the fruit of the Spirit, we will propagate children and protégés of similar character.

> **THE LOUDEST WORDS WE SPEAK ARE THE LIVES WE LIVE.**

A plentiful supply of love, joy, peace, patience, kindness, goodness, faithfulness, gentleness, and self-control (Galatians 5:22–23) is evidence of the Spirit reigning over the flesh in our lives. We will help produce children of a parallel nature. Conversely, hatred, discouragement, hostility, impatience, harshness, fear, shame, inconsistency, and lack of self-control in our lives will propagate insecurities, wounded hearts, and similar behaviour in younger lives.

JESUS AS OUR MODEL

Not only was Jesus the greatest model on earth but He also taught the principle of modeling as one of importance. He followed His

Father's footsteps, saying, "Most assuredly, I say to you, the Son can do nothing of Himself, but what He sees the Father do; for whatever He does, the Son also does in like manner" (John 5:19). Jesus represented His Father, saying, "If you had known Me, you would have known My Father also; and from now on you know Him and have seen Him . . . He who has seen Me has seen the Father" (John 14:7, 9).

Being Christlike is a colossal aim in life. Jesus modeled servanthood, telling His disciples that He did not come to be served but to serve (Matthew 20:28). He modeled prayer, forgiveness, power, authority, and most of all love. Jesus' humility also speaks volumes, seeing as He was the exalted Son of God. The apostle Paul admonishes us in Philippians 2:5–8 to "Let this mind be in you which was also in Christ Jesus . . . He humbled Himself and became obedient to the point of death."

HEALING OF THE HEART

So what can keep us from being good role models to our children? Oftentimes it is the things that were modeled to us, largely by our parents, but also by authority figures, peers, friends, culture, and society. Additionally, issues of our hearts that have wounded us cause ungodly reactions or expressions in our behaviour.

One of the greatest gifts you can give your children is a healthy marriage, and one of the greatest gifts you can give your marriage is a healthy you.

Our dear friends Chester and Betsy Kylstra are the founders of Restoring the Foundations International (restoringthefoundations. org), a ministry of healing and deliverance. My husband, John, and I have received a great deal from this ministry in helping to heal wounds in our hearts and break family patterns we didn't want propagated in our children's lives.

For example, anger was frequently demonstrated in the home I grew up in. My father's father was an angry man, and stories I heard from relatives told of how his anger was unleashed on my father.

In fact, if not receiving physical punishment, my father was locked in the barn or in the basement of his Dutch childhood home for long periods of time. Without knowledge or application of healing of the heart principles, my father grew up to also demonstrate anger towards his wife and children. (I need to add that after much prayer on the part of my mother, and by the healing power of God, my father, now age eighty-four, is greatly changed. He is a loving, peaceful person and is enjoying blessed retirement years.)

The problem was not so much what was done to me in my childhood years but the fact that I reacted wrongly, initially holding unforgiveness toward my father and judging him as being an angry, impatient man. And guess what? I was on track to be just like him. Easily irritated, impatient, angry—the very things I didn't like in my father became traits I demonstrated. Forgiveness, repentance, deliverance, and application of the power of the cross to set me free of these patterns were crucial.

The journey of healing hurts from the past and finding freedom from generational sins or curses is well worth the effort taken to receive prayer ministry or counseling. If you don't do it for yourself, do it for your children!

"Blessed is the man who fears the LORD, who delights greatly in His commandments. His descendants will be mighty on earth; the generation of the upright will be blessed" (Psalm 112:1–2).

MARRIAGE IS A MODEL

The Lord made clear to my husband and me that our priorities were to be the Lord first, each other and our marriage next, our children after that, and then ministry (or vocation). If we put our children before our spouse we are actually propagating disrespect for God's designed order and potentially propagating narcissism in little ones who need to learn proper priorities.

One day, when my husband and I were about to leave for a date night but our son wanted his dad to do something else with him, we tactfully explained to our son that his father's relationship with his mother was of a higher priority than his relationship with his son. Instead of trying to insist on his own desires, I saw a look come over our young son's face of understanding and contentment. Today Judah is married with two sons of his own. He takes his wife on regular date nights, living out the example he observed growing up, whilst modeling it for his own sons.

Speaking of date nights, I have greatly appreciated the fact that almost every week of our married life, my husband has taken me out for one-on-one time. Not only is it wonderful to have uninterrupted conversation, a nice meal that I didn't have to cook, and the undivided attention of my husband, but it is also a statement to our children that we love each other. There is a security in the heart of a child that comes from knowing that their parents love each other and desire time together.

Ephesians 5 speaks of God's design for marriage. The husband is to love his wife as Christ loved the church and gave Himself for her. Wives are to submit to, or be subject to, their husbands. As a man demonstrates sacrificial and unconditional love towards his wife, it is easy for the wife to submit to such a love. It is much easier to submit to a man who is submitted to God.

The last verse of this chapter hits the proverbial nail on the head, "Nevertheless let each one of you in particular so love his own wife as himself, and let the wife see that she respects her husband." I've noticed how respect demonstrated to my husband is very important to him. And a wife longs for the love of her husband. Mutual love and respect in a marriage is a major life model for children. When a son sees the way his father treats his mother, he will, in turn, treat her and other women, including his future wife, similarly. When a daughter watches her mother speak to and about her husband, it ingrains in her how to relate to the opposite sex. Seeing her dad treat her mother with kindness and respect speaks volumes to her about how she should be treated by men and protects her from falling for destructive relationships. When she knows her value, she is much less likely to settle for second best.

I have noticed how unsettling it is for our children if John and I have the slightest disagreement. Demonstrating respectful disagreements and healthy conflict resolution in marriage trains the children watching. I have heard it said you must never argue with your spouse in front of your children. I believe it is good for children to witness healthy conflict resolution in order to enable them to also live out healthy settlements.

A WORD FOR THE SINGLE PARENT

I have great respect for single parents, realizing their job is not an easy one. I have many single-parent friends who take comfort in Isaiah 54:5, "For your Maker is your husband, the LORD of hosts is His name."

The Lord steps in personally as a model of a good husband, sometimes in the most practical ways. My friend Carol Arnott was a single mother of two young sons. When she couldn't open a new jar for lack of strength, she would ask the Lord to help her, and suddenly the jar would open with ease. Her sons watched this. When she married her second husband, John, that supernatural ability to open jars left, as she now had a husband to do it for her!

Single parents model relationship for their children, even in the absence of a spouse. Another friend told me of how the Lord taught her never to speak ill of her ex-husband even though he was not faithful to pay child support, was not helpful with the children when they were young, and left her for another woman. Even though she had justification to speak negatively about this man, she always spoke well of him. The results? Her children all have a good relationship with their father, and he is now much more helpful than he was previously.

In the church, the wider community can step in as models and mentors for children without a second parent. I believe it is ideal that men of the church help a single woman by taking her children to do things a father normally would. Additionally, how nice it would be if women of the church would help a single father teach

his daughters how to apply makeup or get through the trials
of puberty. With the Lord's help and the church's support, single
parents can provide their children the needed modeling.

MODELING THE PURSUIT OF GOD

Years ago the Lord spoke clearly to me, saying, "If you fulfill your
calling, your children will fulfill theirs." It was a directive that my
pursuit of His destiny for me was not just about me but also for the
next generation.

By the grace of God, John and I have had the enormous
privilege of being a part of the leadership of the move of the Spirit
flowing out of Toronto, sustained
through today, nicknamed "The
Toronto Blessing," or "The Father's
Blessing." Because we have been on
staff at Catch the Fire Toronto (formerly Toronto Airport Christian
Fellowship) since 1995, our children

> "IF YOU
> FULFILL YOUR
> CALLING, YOUR
> CHILDREN
> WILL FULFILL
> THEIRS."

have virtually been raised in an atmosphere of revival. Since 2003,
the Lord has given us the revelation of the importance of sustained
prayer and worship in the spirit of the tabernacle of David. We
have been a part of building the house of prayer since that time
and give leadership to the Catch the Fire Toronto House of Prayer.
Thus, our children have also grown up in that atmosphere. They
are now worship leaders, intercessors, singers, and musicians in
the house of prayer. Our younger children often do their homeschool work in the house of prayer. At the time of this writing,
our older daughters are graduating from International House of
Prayer University in Kansas City. Gabrielle is graduating as salutatorian, with a degree in theology and majoring in house of prayer
leadership. Aquila is graduating with a two-year diploma in music.

As much as possible we want our children exposed to the glory
and presence of God. It has helped shape them into who they are
today—radical lovers of God.

May our children find us spending time in prayer each day. May they find us studying the Word of God. May they find us worshiping, listening to worship music in our cars and homes. May they be led by us in diligent church attendance and, most importantly, in radical pursuit of the "pearl of great price"—Jesus Christ.

NEXT GENERATION TESTIMONIALS

Gabrielle Bootsma, our twenty-one-year-old daughter
KANSAS CITY, USA

"Wisdom is justified by her children" (Matthew 11:19). There's no better way to test the fruit your life is producing than through your children. They are the little mirrors constantly running around reminding you of your strengths, weaknesses, habits, etc. Children learn from the example set before them. The wisdom of the decisions you've made in your life, whether past, present, or future, will be fleshed out in the life of your kids.

As a twenty-one-year-old daughter to my parents, I can honestly look at their lives and say "wisdom." Why? I see how the choices they've made to follow the Lord first, to spend time with Him daily, to pray, fast, study the Word, etc., have produced six God-fearing lovers of Jesus.

As Paul said, "Imitate me, just as I also imitate Christ" (1 Corinthians 11:1), so children will look to the authority above them as their example of Christ. Something so encouraging to me growing up was the fact that my parents would never call me to do something that they themselves weren't willing to do. Every morning as I woke, I was told to spend time with Jesus (read my Bible, pray, and journal), but they were unaware of the numerous times I would sneak downstairs and see them in the privacy of their time with the Lord, in tears as they were bent over a passage of scripture. Or the hundreds of hours they spent in the house of prayer, something many would consider foolish; yet their lives and the lives of their children testify that it truly is wisdom. Their actions, far more than just their words, produced the desire in me to obey and spend time with the Lord. To this day, they are my greatest example of Christlikeness, and I continue to imitate them as they imitate Christ.

Georgina Brooks, twenty-two-year-old singer
BATH, ENGLAND

Most days I would come home from school needing to forgive someone—a teacher, classmate, or one of my siblings. One look at Mum, and she knew. She would usher me to sit down and ask me these questions, "How did they make you feel? What did they steal from you?" Together we would pray it through. She didn't just tell me I needed to forgive, but walked it through with me. She showed me how to keep my heart right.

There is one situation in particular where my parents were mistreated, and during these unfair events their response was amazing and provoking. Dad's reaction, though firm and clear, was not harsh or out of anger. It was from a place of sonship. He allowed the Father to fight for him, to take the steering wheel, showing humility and extending grace to the other party. Through it all, I saw by both their words and actions that resting in the strength of our heavenly Father and allowing Him to take the lead is the best and only way. Mum and Dad have a deep relationship with God, never compromising, but always pressing in for more. It's because they had deep roots within the Father that they could react to such a situation with grace and peace.

As great role models, my parents never just told me what was right or wrong, good or bad, godly or ungodly, but they showed me. Although I didn't realize it at the time, as I watched my parents what I saw shaped me into who I am now. My mum and dad caused me to go deeper into the love of God, trusting Him with all I am and will be. I want my relationship with God to be as strong as theirs, so that as they have been to me I can be to others—a role model of Jesus Christ.

Marta Soderberg, twenty-eight-year-old missionary
PEMBA, MOZAMBIQUE

For nearly three years I have been mentored by Heidi Baker. I have daily walked by her side, most often in the dust of Mozambique and a few times in the West.

Heidi is a contagious mentor, and in many situations I make it my quest to follow Heidi's example as she has followed Christ. It comes naturally to ask myself, "How would she have responded in this situation?"

What has impacted my life the most? It is the thousand ways Heidi chooses to humble herself, the way she every single day stops for someone in front of her and loves with her whole heart. It is the way she doesn't have a fake bone in her body, and it's her mind that thinks in a whole different way from anyone I have ever met (always walking in the impossible).

One day when we had a Christmas party in a village in Mozambique, I found a boy shivering in the sand with a high fever. He was tiny, malnourished, and in such a rough state. Heidi's childlikeness came to mind, and I was convinced that all I had to do was to hug and hold this boy in my arms, and he would be healed.

I held him and was interrupted by someone who wanted to talk to me. I laid the boy back on the ground and walked away for a moment. When I turned around the boy had a whole new countenance. He had been too weak to stand to his feet before; his knees couldn't hold him up. Now, all of a sudden, he was running around laughing!

Heidi's example is constantly teaching me to believe like a child, in all simplicity.

2

THE LOVE FACTOR

But the greatest of these is love.
1 CORINTHIANS 13:13

ALL OF US WERE CREATED with a basic need for love. In God's design, families are to be the initial context in which we receive love. Mothers and fathers are called to be the primary ones who demonstrate the love of God to children. Children, learning to receive love from them, can then learn to drink in love from God and others, and love in return. They can face the world with confidence, assured of their worth with a solid foundation. As we seek to raise and mentor children with a passionate heart of love for God as the great commandment states (Matthew 22:37–38), knowing how to cultivate love in their lives is critical.

BASIC TRUST

Psychologist Erik Erikson conducted a great amount of research on human development. He coined the phrases *identity crisis* and *basic trust*. In his stages of psychosocial development[1], Erickson determined that the first stage, from birth to age one, is about *basic trust versus basic mistrust*. In essence, *basic trust* is defined as the belief that the surrounding world is a reliable place. In particular, it is the quality of relationship the child has with the mother that will lead to the forming of basic trust. Affection and nurture shown by the mother reflect their "inner perceptions of trustworthiness, a sense of personal meaning, etc. on the child. If successful in this, the baby develops a sense of trust, which 'forms the basis in the child for a sense of identity.'[2] Failure to develop this trust will result in fear in the baby and a belief that the world is inconsistent and unpredictable."[3]

My oldest sister, Linda, was eighteen months old when her biological mother died of cancer. Linda was raised temporarily by an aunt until our father remarried my mother. Although she was of such a young age when this trauma occurred, Linda's little heart felt the loss of and disruption to her security at the loss of her mother. She recalls having terrible nightmares, seeing snakes and scary people in her room, and crying out in terror.

In almost two decades of ministry, we have known many families who adopted children given up at birth. We have noticed a pattern—without specific prayer and ministry for healing of the little heart that endured such changes, adopted children can struggle with insecurities and mistrust. When they are older, their behaviour can range from striving to be perfect or "earn their way in life" to outright rebellion.

Our learning basic trust at an early age is a foundation on which we learn to trust God and others. It enables us to live life with an open heart, ready to receive and give love in healthy ways.

STORGE

In the Greek language there are four different words for the English word *love*. *Agape* is the unconditional love of God. This love is sacrificial and selfless. *Philia* is the love of friendship and considered a mental love. *Eros* is romantic love, such as between a man and woman. It is sensual and intimate in nature. Lastly, *storge* is familial love, particularly between a mother and child. It is acceptance, affection, and about cherishing one's kindred. *Storge* is demonstrated in three main ways: physical affection, voice intonation, and eye contact.

PHYSICAL AFFECTION

Meaningful touch is important to healthy human development and continued life. Endorphins are compounds produced by the pituitary gland and the hypothalamus, which have pharmacological effects and act as natural analgesics, or pain relievers. Endorphins are excreted during exercise, sexual activity, and meaningful touch.

Ben E. Benjamin, PhD, in an article titled "The Primacy of Human Touch," points out the shocking fact that about a hundred years ago, ninety-nine percent of babies in American orphanages died before they were seven months old.[4] He goes on to qualify that they did not die from malnutrition or disease, but rather from a condition of wasting away called *marasmus,* formed by a lack of touch. "When babies were removed from these large, clean but impersonal institutions to environments where they received physical nurturing along with formula, the marasmus reversed. They gained weight and finally began to thrive."[5]

From 1974 to 1989 Romania was led by a president named Nicolae Ceausescu, who tried to increase the nation's population and industrial production simultaneously by requiring both parents to work and still have large families. As the *Harvard University Gazette* reports, "Many families could not care for their children during weekdays and others abandoned their youngest or least able children to orphanages."[6]

Mary Carlson, a neurobiologist at Harvard Medical School "measured stress in Romanian children raised in orphanages or attending poor-quality day-care centers,"[7] concluding that "the lack of touching and attention stunted their growth and adversely affected their behaviour."[8] She also added that, "they do not form normal relationships with other kids, are unresponsive and fearful, and exhibit behaviour such as self-clasping, rocking, and swaying."[9]

A group of Canadians came into a Romanian orphanage of children aged eighteen months to three years old. What surprised them was the lack of sound in the room. Normally there would be cries, gurgling, or other baby and toddler sounds. What they came to realize is that these little ones had cried with a lack of response to their cries, and had simply stopped trying. Most of these babies and toddlers had some form of developmental delay as a result of a lack of nurture. These children were adopted into Canadian families and many progressed into higher levels of development, but some were not able to return to normal functioning due to the lack of care and nurture.

Ideally, there should be a lavish amount of close contact and touch. A baby in the mother's womb for nine months is used to her warmth, her nearness, and hearing her heartbeat. As much as possible, this should continue after birth. Holding the baby close to the heart, carrying him or her around in a baby sling, caressing cheeks and hair, and holding his or her little fingers are all ways to offer needed touch.

THERE SHOULD BE A LAVISH AMOUNT OF CLOSE CONTACT AND TOUCH.

After our babies outgrew a sling, I would switch to backpack carriers. As a pastor in a church in the midst of a major move of God, with many visitors seeking prayer, I would carry my little ones in the backpack as I prayed for people waiting in long lines.

Personally, John and I are also proponents of having babies sleeping in bed with us, knowing our nearness. We own a king-sized bed, which is helpful to this end. I understand this may not be for all parents. Some have quoted stories of parents who have accidentally rolled on top of babies, smothering them. I'd like to point out that the overwhelming majority of these stories are accompanied by other factors present, such as alcohol or drug consumption by adults, rendering them unable to awaken due to being under other influences.

We transitioned our babies at a certain time to a mattress on the floor next to our bed before putting them into a crib in their own room. At each transition, it was as though the next step "felt right" in our hearts. Although these particular sleep arrangements may not be for all parents, the key principle is the same. A parent senses when the child's heart is ready for each new level of separation, and does not push for it before that.

Beyond those years, children, teenagers, and adults all still need affection. When our son was around fourteen years old, he decided he wasn't so keen on the hugs my husband and I gave him. However, knowing the importance of affection, John and I were not deterred. We still went after him to give him a morning hug, an evening peck on the cheek, or the occasional "love sandwich" we like to give our children (this is where John and I will surround one of our children, both giving a bear hug simultaneously, one on the front and the other on the back—like a sandwich). Soon, Judah forgot he didn't like hugs and was hugging back as usual, and still does to this day as a young adult.

Our fourth child, Phoebe, diagnosed with a developmental delay, often resists affection. Her behaviour began to change at eighteen months of age, something which I believe was connected to a vaccination she received at that time. Her language comprehension and speech deteriorated, her behaviour became more difficult, and her social interactions more challenged. To this day, very rarely will Phoebe initiate affection, and she will often shy away from it. However, again, we have diligently sought to demonstrate affection, knowing the benefits. Phoebe has responded to our perseverance and, at times, initiates hugs. As of the time of this writing we still pray for Phoebe's full restoration and healing.

When I was a child, affection was not frequently demonstrated in my family. However, I wanted this to change in my life and in my parenting. Thus, I needed to forgive those who hadn't shown me much affection and to repent of judging them, which helped to free me from doing (or not doing) the same things (Romans

2:1). I purposely trained myself, through God's grace, to be an affectionate person. Hugs, kisses, and "I love you" are frequent in our household.

VOICE INTONATION

Intonation is defined as the variation of spoken pitch that is used to express the attitudes and emotions of the speaker.[10] Put another way, it is the way someone's voice rises and falls as they are speaking. Have you ever noticed that the intonation of the voice of someone talking to a baby rises, taking on a different pitch? It is actually a form of nurture.

One time I was in a restaurant when two families sat at a table next to mine. When a mother got up to go to the restroom, she handed her baby to a man who must have been the father. This man was large in stature, with a long beard and a copious number of tattoos along his arms. What happened next made me want to burst out in laughter, although I held my tongue. This tough-looking guy suddenly spoke in a high-pitched voice to this little baby, using tender words of affection. It is almost automatic that tenderness is expressed to little ones with a change in voice inflection.

In contrast, angry, loud vocal sounds can cause tension and anxiety, and invoke fear in not only babies but also people of any age. While parents sometimes need to use the authoritative voice that communicates to the child that it is time for productive action, it is very important to eliminate the loud, over-emotional voice expressions that unsettle homes and families, cause rising stress levels, and place wedges in relationships.

EYE CONTACT

Have you ever tried to talk to someone who would not hold eye contact with you? They will look at the floor, look past you, look up at the sky, or worse yet, at their watch! This behaviour can be a reflection of the fact that as little children they did not learn to drink nurture from eye contact with their mothers or fathers.

A newborn baby's eyes can see a distance of nine inches. That also happens to be the average distance from the breast to a mother's face. I believe this is God's perfect design for a baby to look into the eyes of a mother at the important time of breast-feeding. Being the multitasker that I am, I sometimes tried to work on a computer or read a book while breast-feeding one of our babies. However, when those little eyes would look up at me, I knew I needed to put away my tasks and simply stare lovingly into those beautiful eyes, communicating my love for this child.

I have often overheard John saying to one of our children, "Look me in the eyes." It may be when they are receiving correction or when he simply is trying to communicate something of importance. Insisting on clear verbal interaction with loving eye communication is an important part of nurture.

OTHER LOVE EXPRESSIONS

Besides the three main ways infants receive *storge* love, there are numerous other ways to express love to a child. One way is quality time or, in other words, spending focused, enjoyable time with each child, rich in communication. Since we have six children, John and I have noted the importance of spending individual time with each. We call them "dates." We may take them to their favourite restaurant or store, spend time at the park, go for a walk next to the river, or buy an ice cream cone. A child, especially one in a large family, thrives with the individual, undivided attention of a parent.

Love can be expressed in gifts. Since I often travel internationally for speaking engagements, I will always return with a gift for each child. It has to do with communicating that I have been thinking of them while away. Gifts don't need to be expensive, nor should there be unreasonable expectations on a parent to produce all the latest gadgets and designer clothes for children. However, in moderation and in caring thoughtfulness, gifts are a communication tool for love.

Love can also be expressed in acts of service. Mothers are, at times, chauffeurs, nurses, teachers, friends, mentors, advocates, cooks, cleaners, and disciplinarians. Mothers are some of the most

> **A CHILD THRIVES WITH THE INDIVIDUAL, UNDIVIDED ATTENTION OF A PARENT.**

unselfish people. They may eat cold food so the kids are fed first and get on that bus on time. They will go to bed exhausted and still wake up in the middle of the night to comfort a crying child. When I thought about how my mother showed love for me, I know acts of service were her main way of expressing it.

Love is expressed in words. How sad it is to hear stories of those who do not recall hearing their parent tell them they are loved.

A dear young man from Holland came to our school of ministry in Toronto. One of the other students came up to greet him with a hug and said it was like hugging a tree. The Dutch student had a difficult time receiving any form of affection, rarely smiled, was even quite monotone in his speech, and appeared to neither experience joy nor discouragement. He simply came across as emotionally shut down. Later, we found out he had never heard his parents tell him he was loved. Additionally, he was not hugged or given any form of physical affection. Thankfully, in the ministry at our school, he received teaching that helped him to forgive his parents, connect with his Father in heaven, and receive love divinely and from those in the body of Christ. This man came to be one of our ministry interns. It was simply amazing to see the transformation in his life as he frequently smiled, accepted and initiated hugs, and got in touch with his feelings on a deep level.

Verbal expressions of love should be given on at least a daily basis from a parent to a child. Additionally, for every word of correction, I believe there should be seven admonishments of value, worth, and encouragement.

A WORD ABOUT BREAST-FEEDING

When a child receives the affection of the mother, sees her eyes of love, and hears her words of love and voice intonations of the same, that child learns to drink of love. Another important way love is expressed from a mother to a baby is through breast-feeding. Not only are life-giving nutrients imparted in this God-designed act, but also nurture. Psalm 22:9 records it this way, "You made Me trust while on My mother's breasts."

Babies have an innate ability to latch on and suckle at their mother's breast immediately after birth. In fact, if there is a delay in putting the baby to the breast, say for medical reasons, it is more difficult for the child to learn to latch on later. Once there is a latching and suckling, there is an effortless flow of milk. Additionally, there are natural hormones, oxytocin and prolactin, released during breast-feeding that cause the mother to feel tired. The breast milk itself also contains substances that make the baby sleepy. Hence, the baby will often fall asleep at the breast. The peaceful interaction between mother and child is a divine design helping to impart security—a drinking of nurture and love.

I would practice breast-feeding our six children for a much longer duration than the cultural norm. We weaned our babies anywhere from eighteen months to past two years of age. I find it tragic when mothers are eager to end breast-feeding. I would introduce solid foods to our babies by age six months but also continued breast-feeding. Of course, one needs to make this decision for oneself, but when physically possible, I encourage longer breast-feeding. In biblical days, it was normal to breast-feed until the child's third or even fourth year of life. Genesis 21:8 states that Abraham held a celebration of

THE PEACEFUL INTERACTION BETWEEN MOTHER AND CHILD IS A DIVINE DESIGN HELPING TO IMPART SECURITY.

Isaac's weaning. He is believed to have been at least two years old when this occurred. Samuel was old enough to be left at the temple with Eli when Hannah weaned him and dedicated him into service to the Lord (1 Samuel 1:24).

There are women who have had difficulty breast-feeding, who need to return to work quickly or may have a low breast milk supply. Others may have adopted a child they cannot breast-feed. When that is the case, I recommend focused prayer for the child to receive trust and nurture regardless of whether or not they obtain sustenance through breast-feeding. During bottle-feeding, the mother and baby can enjoy the eye contact, sweet words, and tender physical touch that are so nurturing to the baby's heart. We must believe God is bigger—He answers prayer and supplies for every need. I was not breast-fed, and I turned out all right!

How interesting that one of the names of God is *El Shaddai*, meaning "many breasted one," and Jesus stated in John 7:37–39, "'If anyone thirsts, let him come to Me and drink. He who believes in Me, as the Scripture has said, out of his heart will flow rivers of living water.' But this He spoke concerning the Spirit, whom those believing in Him would receive." Learning to receive love and nurture at our mother's breast helps us to learn to drink of God's love. We learn to rest in peaceful assurance that He is faithful, He will come through for us, we are His children, and can abide in His love. We begin to enter rest from striving and self-effort as we learn to drink of Him.

I have heard it said those who have not been breast-fed are more inclined to view the breast as a sexual object. While this could be a factor (indeed, we have a breast-obsessed society), at the core of our young people's vulnerability to hypersexuality is the much broader and profound lack of nurturing love. We were meant to be touched, adored, and lovingly engaged with on multiple meaningful levels by our parents. But when *storge* love is lacking, *eros* goes wild. Young women dressing in such a way as to draw attention to their bodies, young men addicted to pornography, open sexuality in mainstream movies, red-light districts, sex trafficking, and many more expressions of a sexually-driven society can be rooted in a lack of nurturing love in childhood. When humanity hasn't learned to drink of love in the right places, we will search for it in all the wrong places.

FROM LOVE DEFICIT TO LOVE SURPLUS

In a perfect world, our mothers reflect to us the mother heart of God—nurturing, loving, sustaining, encouraging, comforting. Our fathers are to represent the father heart of God—protecting, imparting, directing, and providing. However, oftentimes mothers and fathers have known hurt and a lack of love themselves. They can't give what they don't have.

The good news from God is that even if we are rejected by our mothers and fathers, He will indeed mother and father us. Isaiah 49:15–16 says, "Can a woman forget her nursing child, and not have compassion on the son of her womb? Surely they may forget. Yet I will not forget you. See, I have inscribed you on the palms of My hands." In Psalm 27:10 we find this assurance, "When my father and my mother forsake me, then the LORD will take care of me."

In my mother's generation there was a prevalent teaching that breast-feeding was not important and bottle-feeding was the convenient choice to make. Pictures of me as an infant show a baby drinking from a bottle propped up by a rolled-up towel. Indeed, I struggled for years not only with a lack of love demonstrated by my father but with a shallow relationship with my mother.

As indicated in chapter 1, as we forgive those who have not known how to love us, and ask for forgiveness for our wrong reactions, we can be set free of any love deficits and learn how to tap into the love of God, richly demonstrated to us. His love is demonstrated in so many ways—His Word, His presence, His still small voice, the beauty of His creation, and the love of His people toward us—to name only a few.

At a time when I was particularly dealing with healing of my heart in regards to the Father's love, the Lord sent an older father figure to me in the church I attended who searched me out to hug me every Sunday. At first I tried to avoid this man, but later I realized this was the Lord sending a man to give me the healthy hugs that I had never received growing up. Indeed, my heart began to drink it in.

My husband was also used of the Lord to teach me about unconditional love and acceptance. Before we married, his demonstration of unconditional love, even when I was trying to push him away, revealed to me a part of the heart of God for me. How vast is the Father's love, that it is not conditional on our behaviour or accomplishments (or lack thereof). His love is just . . . there, all the time. First John 3:1a says, "Behold what manner of love the Father has bestowed on us, that we should be called children of God!"

Let's look at specific issues that can arise in this wonderful privilege called parenting and mentoring. These are possible situations where we can remove any potential open doors for darkness. In life there will always be opportunities to overcome, choose God's way, and come higher in character as we triumph with love and nurture.

FAVOURITISM

I once heard the popular Christian speaker Joyce Meyer say that in families of multiple children, mothers often have a more difficult time relating to one particular child. It may be a child who is the same personality as the parent, one who pulls away or tends to shyness, one who is challenged physically, or a particularly strong-willed child. I know someone who had a very difficult relationship with his mother because he closely resembled in appearance the father who abandoned them and didn't help in the raising of the child.

In the farming community where I was raised, sons were the preferred gender. Barns would display, in large painted letters, the name of the farmer and his sons, for example, "Johnson and sons" or "Skinner and sons." Meanwhile, they may have had three daughters, but they were not listed. I felt the favouritism shown to my brothers in such things as the way they were coddled, finances they received, gifts accumulated, and how they were always served first at the dinner table. It was a family joke that my older brother cried when I was born due to the fact that I was a girl. Needless to say, forgiveness, repentance for wrong reactions, and acceptance of my gender were steps I needed to work through.

As parents it is important to identify root causes when we have children we have a harder time relating to, and to make pointed effort to build bridges.

As I mentioned earlier, we have a special-needs daughter. She has taken considerably more time and energy from my husband and me in many areas of parenting. As a toddler she would seem to "bounce off the ceiling"; it took much more effort to keep her occupied, happy, and doing something productive and not destructive. We have noted that the children on either side of Phoebe, her older sister Aquila and younger sister Zoe, have tendencies to pull away, spend longer periods of time in their bedrooms, or keep feelings unspoken. John and I have needed to go after these daughters more, seek to draw them out, and ensure they are not neglected in the rigours of raising a special-needs child close to their ages. I can't say we have done it all correctly but the Lord has been faithful to teach us and give the breakthrough needed as we have pressed into the place of prayer for each of our children.

Loving demonstrations such as affection, time, financial allowances, or words of encouragement should be equally divided among multiple siblings.

DISCIPLINE

Because discipline is an expression of love for our children, it is aptly placed in the chapter on love. "He who spares his rod hates his son, but he who loves him disciplines him promptly" (Proverbs 13:24). "Do not withhold correction from a child" (Proverbs 23:13).

"The rod and rebuke give wisdom, but a child left to himself brings shame to his mother . . . Correct your son, and he will give you rest; yes, he will give delight to your soul" (Proverbs 29:15, 17).

I've heard it said the worst possible state a child can be raised in is one with a lack of boundaries and discipline. Excessive, strict discipline is somewhat better than that, but of course, the best is loving, balanced, clear boundaries and discipline. In a society marching towards permissiveness, abandoning moral absolutes, and careening toward a mentality of "whatever feels right, do it," there needs to be a return to biblical standards of discipline. Proverbs 13:18 states, "Poverty and shame will come to him who disdains correction, but he who regards a rebuke will be honoured." Placing in our children an attitude that embraces correction and a desire to come higher in character and behaviour helps them in life when they need to submit to teachers, work under bosses, be productive in society, and lead their own families.

The parent who yells at the coach who benched his kid for getting one too many penalties, or angrily defends his child to a teacher who sent home a note explaining the need for a detention, is not doing that child any favours in life. How we both administer correction and receive it from others speaks volumes to our children on how they should conduct themselves. "Train up a child in the way he should go, and when he is old he will not depart from it" (Proverbs 22:6).

John and I have taken the stand that we believe discipline can take many forms, such as a look, a corrective word, short time-outs, writing lines fifty times such as, "I will not tease my sister," and when necessary, spankings. Proverbs 22:15 explains that "Foolishness is bound up in the heart of a child; the rod of correction will drive it far from him."

The type of punishment can depend on the child. Some of our children are more sensitive to correction and simply need a verbal warning not to do something twice. Others have necessitated a physical spanking. I've heard it said not to spank a child before age eighteen months and not after ten years old. That may be subject to the discretion of the parent. However, the lack of parental self-control and moral restraint has necessitated child protection laws and children's aid societies. How tragic to hear of a baby shaken so severely by an angry parent that damage is done to the brain, or of correction done in anger turning into abuse.

The problem we have is when society seeks to "throw the baby out with the bathwater" by eliminating corporal punishment in a reaction against abuse. Proverbs 20:11 tells us that "even a child is known by his deeds, whether what he does is pure and right." Have you ever seen a child having a tantrum in a store and wondered if he had ever received a spanking in his life? I understand it is best not to judge (we have had our own store horror stories—particularly with our special-needs daughter). However, taking the child out of the store or the crying toddler out of church to deal privately with behavioural issues is a blessing not only to those around, but to the child who needs loving, consistent discipline. A child's heart thrives with feelings of safety when their parents carry out discipline and instruction consistently.

What about those reading this book who are dealing with disobedience in their children? Of course, prayer is a key to invoking help and wisdom from the Father in heaven. Also, Proverbs 3:12 states, "For whom the LORD loves He corrects, just as a father the son in whom he delights." Because the Father loves us, He corrects us. Because we love our children, we correct them. Often this takes energy and effort. While it may be easier to let things go or turn a blind eye, it is imperative we take the steps necessary to bring correction where needed.

Sometimes tough love is needed. Ungodly music or movies should not be allowed in the home, defiling the home. Household rules must be upheld if older children are to continue to have the privilege of living under the roof paid for them by parents.

May the Lord give us wisdom as parents to hold the line when we know decisions we make for our children are for their good, even if they are not what our children want to hear. The truth is, it takes more effort to correct, instruct, and stand firm for righteousness. It is easier to comply, give in, and avoid conflict. However, in the long term, the "easy way" creates many more difficulties. It robs children of a very important aspect of nurturing love—

> **A CHILD'S HEART THRIVES WITH FEELINGS OF SAFETY WHEN THEIR PARENTS CARRY OUT DISCIPLINE AND INSTRUCTION CONSISTENTLY.**

tough love that doesn't relent in seeking the young one's good. It is worth the effort it takes to intervene, correct, and instruct. As our children grow, we as parents will also reap the reward.

There are some battles we may choose not to engage in—for example, the teenager who wants to colour their hair. Do we let them or not? That may be a personal choice for each parent. I have discouraged our daughters from colouring their hair but did allow the highlighting and lightening my oldest daughter wanted. However, John and I would not allow an unnatural hair colour like blue or purple (thankfully, none of our children asked for that). Then there is the issue of tattoos. My personal stand on that is NO! I will quote Leviticus 19:28, "You shall not make any cuttings in your flesh for the dead, nor tattoo any marks on you: I am the LORD." Thankfully, our children have abided by this directive. But if your children have tattoos—what do you do? Love them unconditionally!

My one daughter insisted on a nose ring for a period of time, quoting Genesis 24:22 as this being a biblical practice. I didn't like the idea but allowed her to get the nose ring. It really did not enhance her beauty, and after much prayer and encouragement, she finally agreed to get rid of it—yeah!

Discipline in each family may take different forms—grounding from going out with friends, no use of the family car for a period of time, writing lines (such as "I will not tease my sister"), or with-holding of allowances or money for certain "want" items. Make it evident that love is the motivator for the discipline—that is key for the child eventually coming around to wisdom, even if it takes years.

In a recent discussion with our daughter Zoe, she kindly pointed out to me that John would consistently give hugs after discipline and tell her how much he loved her, and I was not inclined to do so. Ouch! May you learn from my mistakes! After a time of discipline, it is im-portant to have verbal and physical reaffirmation of love—a hug, an encouragement, and an assurance of full status as a valuable member of the family. In other words, extended isolation in a bedroom or a feeling that they are "in the dog house" is counterproductive.

We are to enjoy our parenting and delight in our children. I remember leaving the hospital with newborn Zoe when the nurse called out after me, "Enjoy your baby." Somehow those words just struck me, and I've never forgotten them. Of course I was to enjoy my baby, every moment of her life, from the changing of diapers to helping with the math lessons to celebrating the wed-

"ENJOY YOUR BABY."

ding. Yet, the pleasure of parenting can be robbed by a child who is not . . . well . . . parented!

Proverbs 23:25 puts it well, "Let your father and your mother be glad, and let her who bore you rejoice."

"Behold, children are a heritage from the Lord, the fruit of the womb is a reward. Like arrows in the hand of a warrior, so are the children of one's youth. Happy is the man who has his quiver full of them" (Psalm 127:3–5).

SIBLING RIVALRY

Psalm 133 says, "Behold how good and how pleasant it is for breth-ren to dwell together in unity! . . . for there the LORD commanded the blessing—life forevermore."

The word *brethren* is the Hebrew word *ach,* which means brother, or immediate relative. Since Jesus is the Prince of Peace and First Peter 3:11 admonishes us to seek and pursue peace, it is important to guard the level of peace in our homes. Sibling rivalry can be a direct obstacle to peace.

Broken relationships among siblings can be a generational curse on families. I have personally seen this in my family line. Two of my uncles did not speak to each other for years. There has been disharmony among some of my own siblings. On John's side of the family there is a marked lack of closeness among the siblings. Thus, John and I have sought to be proactive to not see this pattern propagated in our children. First of all, we have prayed to break any negative family patterns, asking God to forgive us personally for our participation in sibling rivalry, repenting for any judgements, and praying to break any sowing and reaping in this area. We have also sought to deal quickly when we have seen disunity among our children, bringing correction and seeking to foster respect and unity. At times, when there has to be a decision made as to who gets what when, we have deferred to the older sibling, asking the younger sibling to honour the older age of their brother or sister.

There is a need for parents to not compare children nor expect out of one child what another can do easily. And as discussed earlier, parents must avoid favouritism.

Our two oldest daughters are very diverse in their personalities. Gabrielle is much more outgoing, talkative, and apt to go shopping. Aquila is quieter, sensitive, and spendthrift by nature. Both have wonderful gifts, and they are both anointed, lovely women of God. At times, they have also disagreed. Until recently, they have lived together in Kansas City as they both attended university there. Some conflicts arose as to who was going to be in charge of the household affairs in their Kansas City home. As I was praying about what to do, the Lord gave me an idea to write an email to send to them. Amazingly, after they received the email, we heard no more complaints about each other. I thought I would include that letter here. In short, if we ask for wisdom in how to deal with sibling rivalry, the Lord will give it to us. My advice is to not simply let it go but to pursue peace in our homes among our children, and prayerfully, they, in turn, will lead homes of peace in the future.

Dear Gabrielle and Aquila,

When I was growing up on the farm I was the youngest for ten years. That meant some advantages (like not having to work quite as hard as the rest, at least until they left home) and some disadvantages (in working with my siblings, they usually told me what to do). At times there was all out war—like when we would throw eggs at each other in the chicken coup, push someone in the pool, or pummel each other with snow balls. Then there were good times like when I received assistance to lift a heavy hay bale or help to catch my horse in the field. My sister Linda taught me math and how to tell time. I cried when Maria left home because she had a fight with my dad. I still remember Heidi putting Cheez Whiz on her boiled egg every morning. Siebren was a nice brother. I took Joel fishing many times by the creek. Hart . . . well . . . he was always industrious. Those days are gone now, lost in the years of all of us grown and managing our own homes and families.

For whatever reason, God chose me to be one of the younger ones. When my brother Joel came along ten years later, at first I was so happy I had gotten a baby brother like I prayed for. My joy lasted as long as it took for him to come home from the hospital, as I realized I had also gotten bumped from being the baby of the family and subsequent greater attention. Oh, the joy of birth order!

Speaking of birth order, as we know, Gabrielle came in 1993 and Aquila in 1995—as God would have it in His design. Thus, Gabrielle was in Kansas City before Aquila and has managed the household affairs for three years. Has she managed it perfectly? Well, no. Has she done a good job? Yes.

So, while I'm sure Gabrielle appreciates fresh ideas and assistance in managing the house in Kansas City, the fact is when the rubber hits the road or the buck stops or the trump card is pulled . . . Gabrielle is the one to call the shots or give the orders or set the rules, or be the "queen bee" :)

So enjoy your time being sisters living together in harmony. Thankfully, there are no chicken eggs to throw at each other—well, don't reach for the fridge.

Before you know it, the time is gone, you're married and have your own children, who you are trying to convince to get along with each other. Oh and yes, we really want that commanded blessing (Psalm 133).

With Love,
Your Mother

ENTERTAINMENT

I'm going to put a word in here that may stir controversy! In seeking to build a solid love foundation in the lives of our children, I believe one of the largest factors that hinders that cause is television, video games, handheld electronic devices, excessive use of computers—in short, an overindulgence in entertainment. TV screens are tragically used as babysitters, for the toddler right up to young adults. Not only can they input many anti-Christian ideas and philosophies, they can replace face-to-face communication and interaction with parents and among siblings.

John and I have felt so strongly in this regard we simply got rid of our TV many years ago. Instead of a bombardment of images across the massive screen central to many living rooms, we have conversations with our children, play numerous board and card games, go outside or to the gym to play sports or exercise together, walk the dog, or go shopping together. Our children have learned to be good readers, students of the Bible, and ones whose interest is held in conversations with real people and not in wasting their life in a virtual world, playing a game with someone somewhere on another screen.

I once stayed in the home of a family whose twenty-three-year-old son only came out from his bedroom (where he was playing computer games online) to eat. I was there on his birthday, and even then after the birthday cake and candles, he went right back to his bedroom to get back on his computer. I felt grieved in my spirit. Whole portions of this generation are not learning to go after their destiny or interact in the real world. They are overly caught up in a virtual world.

Parents of young children should begin teaching this lesson early. Set a limit on time for use of the TV, computer, and electronics. Monitor closely what music they listen to, what they watch, what they engage in.

We have a rule in our home that our children are not to listen to non-Christian music. There may be some exceptions such as quality songs they occasionally hear that are not of a negative nature. However, we have told them there is plenty of good-quality Christian music that they can choose from. In my van there is always good-quality Christian music playing that our children also find appealing. In our home we often stream the International House of Prayer's free, online, continuous worship and prayer (ihopkc.org/prayerroom).

For entertainment, we purchase many of Focus on the Family's audio Odyssey series or other audio productions (focusonthefamily.com). We do have computers on which we will watch movies we often get from the local library or online. The younger children need to ask permission to watch a movie. John and I use our discernment on movies we haven't seen or go online to get detailed information on the content of a particular movie. We go out to the theatres as a family and like to support quality family or Christian films.

CHILDREN START OUT WITH A SENSITIVE NATURE—A BLANK CANVAS THAT WE ARE PRIVILEGED TO PAINT ON AND GUARD.

At the time of this writing our oldest child is twenty-three years old and our youngest is eleven. We have seen how the standards we set for our children when they were young have carried into their adult years.

Children start out with a sensitive nature—like a blank canvas that we, as parents, are privileged to paint on and guard. As we seek to create in that nature a hunger for the presence of God, to hear His voice and know His love, it is crucial to guard that sensitivity and enhance it through what goes into their eyes, their ears, and their minds.

THE POWER OF JOY

"The joy of the LORD is your strength" (Nehemiah 8:10). Enjoyment of life is part of our inheritance in the Lord. God does not want us depressed, miserable, and going through life with dread. Joy is one of the fruits of the Spirit and "a merry heart does good, like medicine" (Proverbs 17:22).

When there is joy, laughter, and the fun of life flowing in our homes and lives, our children and those we mentor will similarly appreciate and live lives of joy. Through my days in the medical field of nursing, I saw how depression can be a generational problem and literally rob families of their mother, father, or the pleasure of family life. There are times when medical intervention is needed, such as periods when antidepressants can help balance hormones and get someone through a season of difficulty. I also believe there are times of spiritual attacks to steal the joy of individuals that must be warded off through prayer and healing of the roots of discouragement.

We should be determined to enjoy life to the fullest, no matter what our circumstances are. True joy comes from the Spirit within. As I have heard Mike Bickle say, "God is mostly glad not sad."

When the Holy Spirit fell in great power in Toronto in January of 1994, one of the manifestations was unusual laughter. I've seen literally thousands of people in a meeting break out into spontaneous, uncontrollable laughter. Some have rolled on the floor in gales of joy. Others would not be able to walk properly, overcome by the Holy Spirit. The Lord has used this move of the Spirit, which I've been privileged to be a part of, to teach me many lessons. One of them has been just how fun God is. He loves laughter. He loves it when we are full of His presence and full of His joy. Similarly, our homes, filled with joy and laughter, teach children how fun God is and how amazing life is when lived in abundance (John 10:10).

One time our daughter Zoe came home from a friend's house and told us that their family laughed much more than our family. Although I don't encourage comparison, that statement made me more determined to laugh together as a family. John and I were not particularly raised in homes of abundant laughter, and we wouldn't be described as comedians. However, we can help foster joy and laughter in our homes if we desire to. As our children would say, John comes out with corny jokes. I've decided to laugh at them even if they don't seem funny, because any opportunity to laugh is good. I laugh all over again when one of our children says for the fourth time, "When the baby camel was born with no humps, what did his parents call him? Humphrey!"

Our special-needs daughter will sometimes do strange things, whether at home or in public. We have learned it is much more enjoyable to laugh with her rather than be bothered by her behaviour. Yes, we correct when we need to correct, but there are times when you just have to laugh.

Sometimes watching a clean comedy movie, or playing an enjoyable board game, or getting together with friends to simply laugh is just what we need. John and I come from a strong Dutch work ethic background. In other words, we work hard. We found out years ago we needed to teach ourselves to play hard as well. Vacations, times of refreshing, pillow fights, getting away as a family to see Niagara Falls again (it is an hour drive from our home), or whatever creative idea the Lord gives us to foster laughter and fun times, are also very spiritual.

Let's be determined to have the joy of life fostered in our lives and homes. Indeed, even when darkness seeks to cover the earth, God sits in the heavens and laughs (Psalm 2:4).

NEXT GENERATION TESTIMONIAL

Zoe Bootsma, our fourteen-year-old daughter

I have grown up, along with the rest of my family, having no TV to entertain me. People are often surprised and confused when they hear this. They often ask questions like: "How do you entertain yourself?" "What do you do on Saturday mornings?" "Do you just watch movies instead?" "Aren't you always bored?"

Bored. It's such a dreary word. No one should ever have to be bored. Isn't that why, as little children, our imagination is such an important part of us? We can run around and imagine we are anything or anyone we want to be. But if we are always sitting inside watching the results of someone else's imagination, when can we learn to use our own?

I would often complain how all my friends had TVs, and it wasn't fair that I couldn't do what they could do. They could watch as many movies as they wanted, but I could only watch one or two a week. They could play on the computer all the time, but I was only allowed thirty minutes a day. They could always do something that I couldn't do. Now I realize that it was the opposite. They didn't do what I could do.

Having no electronics to always entertain me, I was forced to discover new ways to entertain myself during my free time. On nice days, I would run through a forest next to our subdivision looking for white-tailed deer on my way to visit a farmer's horses. Or, I would walk down the street to the playground and play with other kids. I would pretend with my friends that we were part of the Swiss Family Robinson trapped on an island, and we had to build a house in the trees in order to stay away from all the wild animals that lurked below. Sometimes I would sit on the swings with my eyes closed and imagine I could fly and was floating in the clouds with Jesus, drinking tea.

However, those were just passing childhood activities. I no longer do any of those things, but I do like to read and write. We go to the library once a week to sign out books. I read, and read, and read.

After developing my brain through reading, I found myself far ahead of the rest of my class in literature. It would annoy me when my fellow classmates would stumble on words I found so easy to pronounce and take minutes to read a simple paragraph.

Not only did reading help me in school, it also continued to develop my imagination even after I grew out of play-pretending. I started forming narratives in my mind, and then I turned those narratives into stories on paper. Eventually, paper failed to do the trick and one Christmas my parents blessed me with my own mini laptop. This gift helped me to practice my God-given talent for writing, and someday I hope to publish a best-selling book.

What if I had sat all day watching TV? Not only does it make kids grumpy and ill-behaved, but it saps our imagination until all we want to do is sit inside and play on an electronic device. For me, growing up without a TV was a blessing in disguise.

NOTES

1. Erik H. Erikson, *Identity and the Life Cycle* (New York: W. W. Norton & Company Inc., 1980), 57–58.
2. Ibid., 65.
3. *Wikipedia*, s.v. "Erik Erikson," last modified October 20, 2014, http://en.wikipedia.org/wiki/Erik_Erikson
4. Deane Juhan, *Job's Body: A Handbook for Bodyworkers* (Barrytown, NY: Station Hill Press, 1971), 43.
5. Ben E. Benjamin, PhD, "The Primacy of Human Touch," accessed October 23, 2014, http://www.benbenjamin.com/pdfs/Issue2.pdf
6. William J. Cromie, "Of Hugs and Hormones," *The Harvard University Gazette* (1998): http://news.harvard.edu/gazette/1998/06.11/OfHugsandHormon.html
7. Ibid.
8. Ibid.
9. Ibid.
10. *Wikipedia*, s.v. "Intonation (linguistics)," last modified September 28, 2014, http://en.wikipedia.org/wiki/Intonation_(linguistics)

3

INTERCESSION AND PROPHETIC DECREES

Death and life are in the power of the tongue.
PROVERBS 18:21

MY SISTER ONCE SAID TO me, "When I see someone living aimlessly or struggling to walk out their destiny, I think often a root cause is a prayerless parent." She may very well be right.

It is hard to overemphasize the importance of intercession for our children. Anyone else praying for our kids will be effective and helpful. Yet there is something special about the authority a father or mother holds before the courts of heaven to unleash blessing for their offspring. May we make it a daily discipline to spend time in prayer for our children or those we mentor.

Praying scripture is a helpful tool. The Lord Himself said in Isaiah 55:11, "So shall My word be that goes forth from My mouth; it shall not return to Me void, but it shall accomplish what I please, and it shall prosper in the thing for which I sent it." As we come into agreement with scripture in our prayers and decrees over our children, the power of God's Word is released in their lives.

The prayer of a little-known man in scripture, Jabez, is tucked in the midst of a list of lengthy genealogies in First Chronicles 4. It says in verse 9 that Jabez was more honourable than his brothers. He called on the name of the Lord, and God granted him what he requested. I believe God is longing to make our children honourable and to grant us, and them, what we and they request. We just need to actually ask, seek, and knock. I have found Jabez's little prayer most helpful. Inserting their names, I pray it daily over John, myself, and each of our children (and now our daughter-in-law and grandchildren). For example, "Oh that You would bless Judah indeed and enlarge Judah's territory, that Your hand would be with Judah, and that You would keep Judah from evil, that Judah may not cause pain." It actually takes a while now with six children and two grandchildren and likely more to come! Yet I feel the anointing when I begin my daily prayers this way. I know I'm tapping into the power of the Holy Spirit unleashed on my family as I pray the power of God's Word.

Since prayer unleashes the power and blessing of God, you can look at it as a form of preventative medicine. When our son turned two years old, friends would say, "Watch out for the terrible twos." Somehow that didn't sit right as God's design or truth for our son, and we began to pray for the "terrific twos"—and that is indeed what we got! When our kids began to become teenagers John and I prayed we would have not one day of rebellious teenage years. Out of our six children, five have either passed through the teenage years or are still in them, and we can honestly say we have not experienced one day of teenage rebellion.

As a parent, the temptation when any fever, sore throat, or sickness comes along is to reach for Tylenol or call the doctor. However, I'd like to encourage prayer for healing as the first line of defence. With the Bachelor of Science in Nursing that I hold, I am not against medical help or intervention, and I'm glad for the wonderful Canadian health care system we have. Yet, I'd rather not have to use it!

If your child or those you mentor are struggling with a particular issue, pray about it. God is certainly the best problem solver, Father, and healer. He also loves our children more than we do. Intercession for our children's future, who they will marry, and what the call of God for them is, all unleash divine blessings.

We have a little tradition in our family each time we set out on a travel journey. In the van as we leave, we each pray from oldest to youngest for God's protection and blessing, and for specific details anyone thinks to pray over. On one trip north of Toronto, our daughter prayed to see a moose. Sure enough, we saw a moose at the side of the road! I'm amazed at how this little exercise not only invokes God's blessings but also gives ownership to each child.

"All your children shall be taught by the Lord, and great shall be the peace of your children" (Isaiah 54:13).

PROPHETIC DECREES AND SPEAKING LIFE

The old adage "sticks and stones may break my bones but words will never hurt me," really holds no truth. Words are powerful, especially when spoken over us by authority figures in our lives such as mothers and fathers. Recently I heard a speaker state he was told early in life that he would never amount to anything of significance. Those words marked him for many years as he sought to break that verbal curse off his life and destiny.

James 3 primarily speaks of the destructive, defiling nature of the tongue, comparing it to a small but powerful directive force such as a bit in a horse's mouth or a rudder of a ship. We are admonished to walk in spiritual maturity by bridling our tongues (3:1–2) and not allowing curses in addition to blessings to come out of our mouths (3:10).

It is hard to overemphasize the importance of the words we speak over our children. Indeed, identities and destinies are both formed and destroyed by declarations made by parents. Hopefully, the women reading this book each aspire to be a Proverbs 31 woman. See what it says in verse 26, "She opens her mouth with wisdom, and on her tongue is the law of kindness."

If we ourselves were the recipients of hurtful speech, we must press in to see change in the families we are forming and to end patterns of negativity. I was raised in a family where each sibling had a derogatory nickname. Being the youngest for ten years before my younger brother came along, mine was "runt," as in the little pig who was always trying to catch up to the rest. That and various other negative labels left me warring for the truth of who I really was and the destiny God had for me. Thankfully, through the power of forgiveness, repentance for believing lies, and the power of

> **IDENTITIES AND DESTINIES ARE BOTH FORMED AND DESTROYED BY DECLARATIONS MADE BY PARENTS.**

the Holy Spirit to break the effects, I was able to receive healing and see the labels broken from my life. My journey of learning to place my tongue under the leadership of the Holy Spirit has been a long one but well worth the effort.

The first step, closely linked to our thought life, is to stop speaking negativity. Humbling ourselves and apologizing to our children when we do err in our words or actions always goes a long way toward restoration—even if the apologies are given years later.

I remember Jack Frost, a speaker on the message of the father heart of God, telling of when the Lord so impacted his life, he knew he needed to apologize for being a harsh, demanding father to each of his children. The resulting restoration of relationship was life-altering for his children.

In a quest for raising children of excellence, there must be an avoidance of negative character statements. Instead, needed directives over certain behaviours or patterns can be given. For example, instead of stating, "You are so rebellious; you never do what I say," the admonishment could be, "You didn't clean your room like I asked you to. Please do so right now." Similarly, we didn't allow our children to speak negative statements over themselves or others. For example, our daughter Aquila was overheard saying, "I'm no good at math." We quickly corrected this negative statement, asking her to repent for saying it. John and I told her she could say she needed help with her math work, adding, "You are clever, and as you apply yourself, you will understand these concepts." Aquila graduated from that grade with a ninety-eight percent in math, so we saw firsthand the power of helping our children change their speaking.

Ending negative statements is important, but it is only half of the equation. Speaking positive or life-giving words is what helps release the power of blessing.

The Lord tells us in Deuteronomy 30:14–15 and 19, "But the word is very near you, in your mouth and in your heart, that you may do it. See, I have set before you today life and good, death and evil . . . I call heaven and earth as witnesses today against you, that I have set before you life and death, blessing and cursing; therefore choose life, that both you and your descendants may live." This passage (and many more like it) shows the power of the Word of God in our mouths, spoken over ourselves and over our children, to release life. That can take the form of declaring the written Word of God over them and, I believe, the prophetic word of God.

Even when they were still in the womb, John and I would begin to declare life over our children. Each day of our children's lives, we have spoken life-giving declarations over them, whether face-to-face or simply in our prayer time for them.

Years ago, I developed a mixture of scripture and other life-giving words which I would declare face-to-face over my children each day. Even today I will do so regularly over Skype with our older children who no longer live at home. It is this, "You are the head and not the tail. You are above and not beneath. You will lend to many nations and never have to borrow. Everything you put your hands to prospers and succeeds. You are blessed and a blessing everywhere you go. The fruit of the Spirit lives inside of you. You walk in favour with God and man. Doors from the Lord open for you. You are smart and understand your schoolwork. You will marry only whom the Lord has for you. You are a Bootsma—you are set apart for righteousness."

I'm amazed at how this little admonition has impacted our children and how they have learned to value the significance of their parent declaring such things. Our oldest son, Judah, now declares it over his two little sons. A university classmate of our daughter Gabrielle heard me declaring it over her during a Skype conversation. He wrote it down to declare over himself (except the Bootsma part). He then proceeded to tell the entire class about the declarations, and they asked Gabrielle to declare it over them! Truly children, teenagers, young adults—really anyone—are longing for the power of blessing.

Scriptures such as the following reveal we are to war for our destiny in the Lord and to see fulfillment of the prophetic words spoken over us, and to war for the prophetic words and destinies of our children and those we mentor: "God . . . calls those things which do not exist as though they did" (Romans 4:17).

"This charge I commit to you, son Timothy, according to the prophecies previously made concerning you, that by them you may wage the good warfare" (1 Timothy 1:18).

Declarations are a form of prayer in which we simply speak out those things we know are in agreement with God. I have many detailed declarations I say/pray over myself, John, our children, our church, those in our sphere of influence, and even over the nation of Canada. We also have detailed declarations we make over each of our children according to the prophecies over their lives, needs they may have at a certain time, and/or desires we have for them. One of my general declarations in my daily prayer life over all our children is, "Our children are passionate lovers of God. They pursue the Lord, live the great commandment and the Great Commission. They marry only whom the Lord has for them and they walk in fullness of destiny. Their spouses are passionate for the Lord and walk in fullness of destiny. Our children grow in favour with God and man. Doors from the Lord open for them. The Lord protects John, myself, and our children. We walk in full-ness of health and healing and prosper in all things of the Lord. No weapon formed against us shall prosper, and every tongue that rises against us in judgement, You shall condemn. "'This is the heritage of the servants of the LORD and their righteousness is from Me,' says the LORD' (Isaiah 54:17)."

We have seen firsthand the effects of these words of blessing. Our son Judah is both the youth pastor in the church where John and I formerly ministered and a worker in the office of a cell phone tower company. Recently a man in that company told me the owner, who hired my son, said he hired Judah partly because he wanted the favour that is on Judah's life to be in his company. Doors have opened for our children where we have seen the hand of the Lord in favour. For example, of our three oldest children, they have received six different scholarships in schools of ministry, missions schools, or in university. That is favour!

If our children are struggling with any health issue we will declare the healing and most often see it manifest in the natural. Our youngest daughter, Glory Anna, was born with a protrusion in her mouth, which we found out was called a ranula and could only be repaired surgically at a later age. We didn't like the idea of our daughter needing to undergo surgery, so we began to pray and decree the ranula would go and healing would come. It took four years, but suddenly the growth disappeared, and Glory Anna did not need surgery.

Our daughter Gabrielle was given a medical diagnosis of a growth or tumour on her thyroid. A naturopathic doctor was con-vinced it was cancerous, an ultrasound showed a significant sized growth, and we were told she needed surgery to have her thyroid completely removed. It was a call to prayer, fasting, and declaring healing over our daughter. Our house of prayer team, loving friends, and family warred with us. A battle in my heart to come into faith and not fear was greatly aided by daily declarations of Gabrielle's healing.

Weeks later, during another ultrasound for the purposes of obtaining a biopsy, a miracle was revealed. The tumour had completely disappeared with no medical intervention!

When one of our daughters began to lament she didn't have enough friends, I admonished her to take ownership herself to decree new, godly friendships in her life. She did so and within a short period of time, a family with a girl her age moved near, and another girl befriended her at church. Truly we change the lives we live when we change the words we speak.

LIVING PROPHETIC DESTINY

"For many are called, but few chosen," Jesus said (Matthew 20:16). What does that mean? I believe it alludes to the fact that we, as believers, have a great call from God for our lives, but few are actually seeking and choosing to live it out. Some of that means paying the price of faith, obedience, and warring for our destiny and for the destiny of those around us.

The call of God on our life or the destiny of God on our children is conditional upon our (or their) response.

We can see the conditional aspects of prophecy or destiny in many passages of scripture. The life of Solomon would be an example. The Lord actually appeared to Solomon twice. The first time He appeared to him in a dream and asked Solomon what he wanted (1 Kings 3:5). Solomon had replied he wanted an understanding (literally means hearing) heart to judge or lead the people. The Lord was pleased with such a request and gave Solomon not only great wisdom, but also riches and honour. The

> **TRULY WE CHANGE THE LIVES WE LIVE WHEN WE CHANGE THE WORDS WE SPEAK.**

second visitation is recorded in First Kings 9 after Solomon dedicates the completed temple to the Lord. Here the Lord spells out the necessary price of obedience.

> "Now if you walk before Me as your father David walked, in integrity of heart and in uprightness, to do according to all that I have commanded you, and if you keep My statutes and My judgments, then I will establish the throne of your kingdom over Israel forever, as I promised David your father, saying, 'You shall not fail to have a man on the throne of Israel.' But if you or your sons at all turn from following Me, and do not keep My commandments and My statutes which I have set before you, but go and serve other gods and worship them, then I will cut off Israel from the land which I have given them; and this house which I have consecrated for My name I will cast out of My sight." (4–7)

Notice the conditional aspects of this prophecy.

Sadly, even though the Lord appeared twice to Solomon, giving him wisdom and blessings, Solomon took one thousand wives and concubines, whom he "clung to in love" (1 Kings 11:2). His foreign wives turned away his heart from the Lord. The Lord became angry with Solomon, and this was the beginning of the downfall of the Davidic dynasty. Solomon and his descendants did not see the fulfillment of the word from the Lord due to disobedience and straying from the God-given path for them.

A three-part remedy for overcoming evil is given in Revelation 12:11, "And they overcame him by the blood of the Lamb and by the word of their testimony, and they did not love their lives to the death." Besides what has been accomplished for us on the cross and our wholehearted abandonment, this passage also cites our testimony as a part of living as an overcomer. The word *testimony* means witness, historical attestation, or evidence. What is the witness or testimony we speak about ourselves and our children? Our words impact those around us, either helping them to walk in greater victory or hindering their ability to overcome. Constant belittling or pointing out faults brings discouragement, which weakens the spirit. Encouragement and declarations of life build us up and help us overcome.

Our words (which stem from our hearts and belief systems) are powerful catalysts or deterrents to prophecies coming true over our lives and the lives of our children. Heaven and hell are both looking for human agreement. Who will we agree with in our minds and in our mouths? The implications are death or life (Proverbs 18:21).

> ## WHO WILL WE AGREE WITH IN OUR MINDS AND IN OUR MOUTHS?

NEXT GENERATION TESTIMONIALS

Judah Bootsma, our twenty-three-year-old son
STRATFORD, CANADA

It's no small thing to have your parents speak a blessing over you every morning as you get ready for school, go out the door, or end a phone call. The same prayer always resonated with me, "You are the head and not the tail, above and not beneath. You will lend to many nations and never have to borrow. Everything that you put your hands to will prosper and succeed. You are highly favoured of the Lord. You are a Bootsma—set apart for righteousness . . ."

To the degree you hear it, you start believing and living up to those words. Even now, as I have two kids of my own, I say it over them as I go out the door to work. I notice how the trend is already setting. My two-year-old is bold, smart, a leader, and talks with authority and wisdom way beyond his age.

Six years ago I started saying decrees over my life. I started calling forth qualities in my life, in my future wife, in who I am, and who I was to become. I saw those words resonate and take shape in my life and what I did. I stated things like, "I am free of strongholds and addictions." It brought such freedom to areas in my life. I also decreed, "I am saving myself for my wife and she is saving herself for me." Guess what? It happened!

Bethany Bootsma, Judah's wife
My parents operated under the premise, "If you can't say anything nice, don't say anything at all." My dad was always very uplifting in telling his daughters they were beautiful, kind, patient, etc. My mom would often say, "Your most enduring quality today was . . . generosity," (or whatever she saw that day). I feel the impact of those words today and now speak and teach similar encouragement to my sons.

Kailyn D'Orazio, twenty-four-year-old worship leader and photographer
STRATFORD, CANADA
I have witnessed firsthand the power of words. I used to wonder why things in my life were not going the way that I wanted them to. I used to wonder why everyone else around me was seeing the things they wanted to see happen and I wasn't. Interning under Patricia (otherwise known affectionately as my "Mama Boots"), I heard her speak quite regularly on prophetic decrees and how your words—and God's word—can affect your life. She spoke about how we can actually decree and declare the good things of God to come to pass in our life. She taught that writing these things down and declaring them over my life on a daily basis would allow my heart and mind to be able to focus on the good things of God, His promises, and what He says about my life. She shared how these things would become a reality in my life.

I started by writing out Bible verses and putting my name in them and reciting them over myself. I then started taking my prophetic words that people had spoken and the promises of God and pulling key phrases out and reciting those too. Things like "my oneness with the Lord defines me," "God will grant me the desires of my heart because He loves me," "I will come into the call, destiny, and fullness of that for which the Lord has chosen me," and "I will have fullness of joy all my days." I declared promises and truths that I could set my heart and mind on. I even started writing down things about my future husband and children. Things like, "My husband is a passionate, God-loving, God-fearing man who will love me as Christ loves the church." And, "My future children will serve the Lord all the days of their lives."

Well, guess what? It worked. It really, truly worked. These truths are seated deep in my heart and I am now living out of a place of knowing who I am and Whose I am. My life is wonderful and my relationship with God is strengthened and deepened on a daily basis as I set my heart and mind on His Word and His promises. I am getting married this September to a wonderful man who is passionately in love with God and loves me exceptionally well, and our future children will serve the Lord all the days of their lives! I now walk in a place of favour and identity that I struggled to walk in before.

Marta Soderberg, twenty-four-year-old missionary
PEMBA, MOZAMBIQUE

For over two years I lived with the Bootsmas. Almost every morning I would wake up to John and Patricia decreeing and speaking truth over their children as they walked out the door to school. (My room was next to the hallway).

One morning I felt God said, "Do you get it yet? If John and Patricia decree so passionately and faithfully over their children every morning, how much more do I want you to wake up to My decrees over you, My beloved?" I love waking up to hearing the Father's voice decreeing His truth over me, and I love to agree with Him. Since I had this revelation of the Father speaking who I am, every time I open up my eyes in the morning, I feel like I live from a place of royalty and worth that I sense no need of proving.

Cerys Gemma, twenty-six-year-old School of Ministry leader
WALES, UNITED KINGDOM

Recently, I moved to Toronto to attend the Catch the Fire Toronto School of Ministry. One of our speakers was Patricia Bootsma. She taught us about the importance of speaking godly, scriptural declarations over our lives. I knew this was revelation I needed to apply to my life.

The areas I particularly needed breakthrough in were health and finances. For many months I was suffering from a strange illness for which the doctors said there was no medical explanation. I also struggled with fear for many years. Regarding finances, I had been in a spiral of debt since I was eighteen. I owed a lot of money on my credit cards and for a bank loan.

After hearing about decrees, I spent time with the Lord and figured out what my decrees should be. I then started to speak them out in faith every day. Some of my decrees included: "He was beaten so we could be whole. He was whipped so we could be healed (Isaiah 53). I expect not to be ill, believe I'm forgiven, accept I'm good enough, trust God's enough for me." "I'm fearless and have good self-discipline, 'For God has not given us a spirit of fear and timidity, but of power, love, and self-discipline'" (2 Timothy 1:7, NLT). "I'm a good steward of finances. 'He will provide and increase your resources and then produce a great harvest of generosity in you'" (2 Corinthians 9:10, NLT).

In a couple months, I started to see significant breakthrough. First, my health was getting better and my energy levels dramatically increased. I also saw fear go from my daily life. Regarding my financial struggles, I had revelation about my attitude toward money. God asked me to trust Him and stop meeting my own needs by putting things on a credit card. My perspective and heart were transformed. I continued to declare, pray, and trust. One day, I got a call from an unexpected source. It was a person saying they wanted to pay all my debt! God came through for me. He abundantly provides for my needs.

4

THE POWER OF BLESSING

That you may inherit a blessing.
1 PETER 3:9

THE POWER OF BLESSING IS clearly demonstrated in scripture, starting in the garden of Eden when God blessed Adam and Eve, commanding them to be fruitful, multiply, fill the earth, and subdue it (Genesis 1:28). The Abrahamic covenant blessing given by God, recorded in Genesis 12 and repeated in Genesis 17, was called an "everlasting covenant" (Genesis 17:19), was to be passed on through Isaac and through the generations, and is applicable still today. Parental blessing, particularly from fathers to children, was considered of monumental importance. The ceremonial blessing Isaac gave to Jacob (Genesis 27:29) could not be taken back, although an anguished Esau wanted that blessing to be his. Jacob (Israel) in turn prophetically blessed his sons (Genesis 49), setting them on track to fulfill their God-given roles as leaders of the twelve tribes of Israel.

Father God Himself spoke in an audible voice over Jesus His Son as He entered the waters of baptism, stating, "You are My beloved Son; in You I am well pleased" (Luke 3:22). Please note that at this point Jesus had not fasted, performed any miracles, or even preached one sermon. This was an unconditional recognition of identity and blessing not contingent on performance.

Identity is about answering the question, "Who am I?" and destiny is about answering, "Why am I here?" When answered by God or by Satan, they are two totally different answers. Remember, heaven and hell are both looking for human agreement.

Basically, blessing is God's impartation of identity and destiny, and cursing is Satan's impartation of identity and destiny. Put another way, blessing is empowerment to succeed in what is really important in life, under God's favour and protection, and cursing is empowerment to fail. As a parent we have a God-given responsibility to place our children under the fountain of the Father's blessing. We are to be His agents of blessing.

LIFE STAGES

Craig Hill (familyfoundations.com) has written insightful books, such as *The Ancient Paths* and *Bar Barakah*, related to the power of blessing, which John and I found very helpful as applied to our parenting. He describes seven crucial stages in life when blessing is necessary in order to impart a sense of identity and destiny.[1] "At each stage God has assigned certain persons, especially parents [but also mentors], to bless us through words, deeds and ceremonies. These blessings become divine deposits in our hearts, and represent essential affirmation about who we are and where we are going . . . When we possess them in abundance we prosper in life without striving. When they are absent, we struggle in life."[2]

Terry and Melissa Bone (powerofblessing.com), Canadian Christian leaders and authors of *The Family Blessing Guidebook*, took Craig's teachings and developed a series of life questions that corresponded to each stage. These questions help determine the divine deposit of blessing we need in our soul and spirit at each developmental stage so one can mature into rightful identity and destiny.[3]

Stage of Life	*Major Life Questions*
1. Conception	Am I welcome in this world?
2. Pregnancy	Is there a safe place for me in the world?
3. Birth	Will my needs be met in this world?
4. Early Childhood	Who can I trust in this world?
5. Teen Years	Do I have what it takes to make it in this world?
6. Adulthood	What am I called to do in this world, and who will share my journey?
7. Senior Years	Am I still needed in this world?[4]

CONCEPTION: AM I WELCOME IN THIS WORLD?

Life truly begins at conception when the spirit of the child is imparted, rather than on the birthday. Therefore, the first time the little one needs a blessing is the moment the announcement comes that the mother is expecting. Seeds of rejection can be sown at conception, such as how the child was conceived and the reaction of parents at receiving the news. Ideally, parents should speak over the womb of the mother with blessings to the little life forming within.

John and I were married only two months and I had just begun my last year of university when I began to suspect I was pregnant. I remember kneeling on the floor of our apartment telling God this would not be a good time to be pregnant. I was in a wrestling-like prayer time listing all the reasons why I should not be pregnant yet: we just got married, I needed to finish my degree, I wasn't sure I was ready for the added responsibility. All the while I could feel God's love and patience with me, but I felt He wasn't moved by my excuses. I ended that time with this familiar surrendering statement, "Nevertheless Lord, let Your will be done, not mine." Immediately, I felt incredible peace sweep over me, and at that moment I knew (not suspected, knew) that I was pregnant. When it was later confirmed by a doctor's visit, John and I began to speak blessing and welcome to the baby in my womb, praying for cancellation of any effects of my initial hesitation. Judah was born two weeks before my graduation from university. He is a delight, a man of God, and was born in God's perfect timing.

PREGNANCY: IS THERE A SAFE PLACE IN THE WORLD FOR ME?

Recent studies have proved pre-born children are affected by their mother's emotions, whether good or bad. "The home environment and the mental, physical and emotional states of a mother serve to answer this life-question for the baby."[5] The unborn child can also hear the mother's voice by four months of gestation.

I sought to avoid sources of stress while pregnant and to keep myself in a place of peace, rest, and the presence of God as much as possible. John and I made it a daily practice to bless the baby in my womb. We would speak specific words of blessing such as blessing the child with good health, a love for the Lord right from the womb, and a sensitive spirit to the presence of God. We also listened to the voice of God for each of our children and prayed over their destiny as the Lord revealed it to us. For example, while pregnant with Judah, the Lord spoke to me to read the Bible out loud over the baby in my womb each day, as he was going to be a man of the Word of God as well as a man of worship. After birth, it was a humorous observation that as a crawling baby Judah would find the

> **JOHN AND I MADE IT A DAILY PRACTICE TO BLESS THE BABY IN MY WOMB.**

Bibles in our home (somehow he always knew the difference between a book and the Bible) and would proceed to eat the pages. Later, Judah's love for the Word of God became evident and still is to this day.

We have observed our babies were all very peaceful, joyful, and a pleasure to parent. I believe the level of peace we sought to live in, as well as the blessings spoken while in the womb, gave our children a solid foundation even before birth.

I'd like to add that John and I never wanted an ultrasound to find out the gender of our children ahead of birth as we enjoyed the surprise. There were two of our children where we just knew the gender ahead of time—our first two. However, I'd like to caution parents against relying on their sense for the gender and going out to buy blue or pink outfits, or speaking according to a certain gender, until you have the confirmed gender either by ultrasound or at birth.

BIRTH: WILL MY NEEDS BE MET IN THIS WORLD?

Immediately after birth each of our children was placed in John's or my arms and we began to speak blessing to our babies, telling them how much they were loved and welcomed. At each of our six births we wept with joy.

As addressed in chapter 2, how babies are held, touched, and fed, as well as the words they hear and the manner in which they are spoken, teach them whether or not their needs will be met in life.

I know there are different schools of thought on strict schedules for feeding, napping, and other daily activities. While I value schedules and recognize they are easier on the parent, I would also breastfeed my babies when they were hungry, put them to nap when they were tired, and seek to help them learn to sleep well during the night, though I also responded to their cries. The truth is you need to be led of the Lord for what your parenting should look like; lean on your God-given instincts and gut feeling. I would caution against an overemphasis on a strict adherence to schedules.

The truth is, from being in ministry and even traveling the nations with babies with me in airplanes, hotels, and conference centres, I have found a baby will adapt well in almost any situation when given the love, nearness, and responsiveness of a mother. I remember being on an airplane from Toronto to Sydney, Australia (a twenty-hour flight), with my five-month-old Glory Anna in my arms. When we landed in Australia and were disembarking, the

man in the seat in front of mine saw my baby and exclaimed in
surprise, "I never knew there was a baby behind me on that long
flight!" That is grace! That is a peaceful baby!

BABY DEDICATIONS

We publicly dedicated each of our children to the Lord in a short
ceremony in our church. Baby (or toddler or child) dedications are
a way for parents to bring their child before the Lord and before the
church family they are a part of, dedicating their child to the Lord.
There is often a blessing pronounced over each child by a pastor or
leader, and a certificate is often given as a physical symbol of this
decision. As pastors, John and I also encourage the congregation
to see themselves as an extension of the spiritual family that helps
in the raising of a child. That may look like praying for the child
and family, helping with practical needs, serving in the children's
department, or other expressions. The saying "It takes a village to
raise a child" can also be stated, "It takes the family of God to raise a
child." I highly recommend parents publicly dedicate their children
to the Lord in whatever church or fellowship of believers to which
they belong.

EARLY CHILDHOOD: WHO CAN I TRUST IN THIS WORLD?

During the years of growth from toddler to pre-teen, Terry and
Melissa teach, you will learn which relationships are safe and which
are not. A foundation of basic trust needs to be poured into a child's
personality during those years for that child to grow in relationships later in life. Regular spoken blessings are important in these
formative years.

A WORD ABOUT EDUCATION AND OUR CHILDREN

I'm going to add at this point, John and I have chosen the more difficult but greatly rewarding task to homeschool our children rather

than send them to a public school. Here is another controversial and strong statement I will make: I was determined to have my children not set foot one day in a public school system. I bless the teachers, the students, and those who labour in the public school system. Our stand has everything to do with the way we knew the Lord wanted our children to be formed and fashioned for the purposes of God for them. We knew we, or those who are like-minded believers in Jesus, were the best ones to paint on the wide open, precious canvas of our children's lives. I have heard it stated that we need to send our children into the public system to be missionaries or light bearers. I do not agree with that premise for our young or teenage children. Once a life is formed and solidified in Jesus, let's send them out as missionaries and agents of life—not when they are impressionable, as they are at such tender, crucial ages. I know godly teachers making a difference in the school system. I'm thankful for them, bless them, and am glad they are making a difference. I also hear from them how hard it can be in that mission field. At least they are adults, solidified in their faith and taking their stand from that vantage point.

While living in Stratford, Ontario, for eight years, an amazing Christian school (up to grade eight) was near our home. It had incredible Christian teachers, and the principal attended the church we pastored. It was at that time we had peace to release our children into school outside of the home. Once the older children graduated from grade eight, with no quality Christian high school in a reasonable distance from our home, I returned to homeschooling. Our three oldest children all graduated from homeschool high school. They have also all gone on to colleges or universities. Indeed, our daughter Gabrielle just graduated from four years in university as salutatorian, with the second-highest marks in her entire class. Obviously, she learned well the basics in homeschooling!

Once, on vacation, I picked up Tim Tebow's book *Through My Eyes* and was impressed to read how this star college football player, then in the NFL, was raised as a homeschooler. His mother's influence as his teacher helped to solidify a faith that he is not ashamed to have broadcast on major media outlets. The doors the Lord has opened for him are great, but he has held the line in his beliefs with the solid foundation he was given.

After being in that Christian school for eight years with a one-on-one worker paid for by the government, our special-needs daughter is now in the Catholic school system in a special program for those with developmental delay. I am grateful for those in the Catholic system. What I have seen is an acknowledgement of Jesus, His divinity, and righteousness.

CHURCH ATTENDANCE

I am very grateful to my parents for taking me to church every Sunday of my childhood. Even though, at age sixteen, I switched churches to attend one that taught and practiced the fullness of the Spirit, I am so grateful for the foundation I had of attendance in a fellowship that honoured God as God, Jesus as His Son come in the flesh, and the authority of the Word of God. Sometimes I miss the hymns I used to sing as a child in church, and I still remember the words and melodies. As the collection plate was passing by, I learned how to give to God. I learned the security of the fact that I was a part of a large body of others who also believed in Jesus.

"And let us consider one another in order to stir up love and good works, not forsaking the assembling of ourselves together, as is the manner of some, but exhorting one another, and so much the more as you see the Day approaching" (Hebrews 10:24–25).

When parents regularly attend a church or fellowship of believers and instill in their children at an early age the value of Christianity in community, it goes a long way in forming good habits—the child who becomes a teenager who becomes a young adult will have the instilled value of attendance in Christian community. Ideally, fathers and mothers (or at least one parent) should bring the children to the service. I have noticed many times if a father does not attend church along with his wife and children, at some point that child will determine that if church isn't good enough for Dad, it isn't good enough for them. How important to set a good example of Christian discipline. The "church of the unchurched" or those who have left their local fellowship of believers yield many negative effects on a child as the years unfold. These children tend to wander spiritually like a ship tossed by wind with no anchor of relationship in a solid family of believers. If they are children of unbelieving parents, attending church through a Sunday school program, a Vacation Bible School, or a Christian summer camp, can be life-changing for them. Studies have proved that the majority of adults who have a faith in Jesus dedicated their lives to Jesus as children.

I was twelve years old and had just started grade seven, attending a newly formed Christian school. I will never forget my teacher, Mr. Dejeger, who clearly explained to our class the need to be born again. In the month of October, I cried myself to sleep for nearly the whole month. I wanted to know what it meant to be born again. After that month, I just knew that I knew I was born again (of course, it normally doesn't need to take a month).

How important it is to impart truth to our children in these formative years, including their need for being a relational part of a body of believers.

TEEN YEARS: DO I HAVE WHAT IT TAKES TO MAKE IT IN THIS WORLD?

Puberty brings monumental transition, not only physically but emotionally. Insecurities can manifest even as the body is changing and hormones are raging. The development of emotional maturity and confidence is particularly needed in these years. Thus, the blessings of parents over children or teens as they enter into puberty years are very important. Added insight for this age group is discussed in the following section called Bar and Bat Barakah.

I made one big blunder in parenting when I forgot to give one of our girls a pre-puberty talk so she would know what to expect before it arrived. Indeed, puberty struck earlier than I anticipated! I'd like to encourage moms and dads, or at least moms, to give their girls the puberty explanation in good time before it occurs. How we approach this important threshold is important to how our girls will view it—not as "the curse" some call it but a time of blessing in God's order of how He designed the body to function. Similarly, parents (or dads) need to speak to sons in preparation. If a single parent, the gender is not as important as having the discussion.

The talk on reproduction, sex, and the sanctity of marriage is best coming from a loving parent rather than peers, the movie screen, or some magazine. It may come at the same time puberty changes are explained, or be a separate discussion. I remember my father telling me to watch the cows as they mated. Somehow that wasn't particularly appealing or informative!

John and I recently had our last "birds and bees" discussion with our youngest child, our eleven-year-old daughter Glory Anna. We both contributed to a simple explanation of human anatomy, menstruation, and then the sexual act to be reserved for marriage. It was a precious time where we ended with prayer and hugs knowing an impartation of our values was clearly communicated and received.

ADULTHOOD: WHAT AM I CALLED TO DO IN LIFE? WHO WILL SHARE MY JOURNEY?

Helping our young-adult children navigate the waters of vocational calling and relationships with our blessing helps set them on a solid path in life. I will address dating versus courtship in chapter 8. We desire our children to marry those the Lord has for them, ones who will share their spiritual journey. Young adults and adults are looking for those they can share with journey of life with. For those called to the single life by choice or chance, God intends to bring alongside them close friends who understand them and share the dream of who they are to become. What a pleasure it is as a parent to give blessing to our children and their fiancés, and then to them and their new spouses in the marriage ceremony.

SENIOR YEARS: AM I STILL NEEDED IN THE WORLD?

Terry and Melissa Bone describe the senior years this way: "Everyone who has reached their senior years needs to know that they are still needed. In biblical times elderly people stopped working in the fields and took up their positions of honour in the city gates. This was a place of authority."[6]

Recently, I had a discussion with two of our children explaining the importance of giving honour to the older generation. This can be reflected in many ways—visiting the elderly in a retirement home, getting up so an older person can take your seat on a bus, addressing the elderly in a respectful manner, or offering to cut their lawn or shovel the snow in their driveway. Modeling and teaching our children to honour the elderly is one way we can help bless the generation that has gone on before.

What is the ideal answer to each of the above questions? A blessing.

Even if we were not blessed by parents as we passed through each of these life stages, how wonderful it is that we can receive the blessings of our Father in heaven who heals wounds, closes gaps, and brings fulfillment of identity and destiny.

"Blessed be the God and Father of our Lord Jesus Christ, who has blessed us with every spiritual blessing in the heavenly places in Christ" (Ephesians 1:3).

BAR AND BAT BARAKAH

In the Jewish tradition an important coming-of-age rite of passage occurs at age thirteen for a boy and age twelve for a girl. For a boy, this ceremony is known as his bar mitzvah. That term means "son of the law (or commandment)." For a girl it is a bat mitzvah or "daughter of the law (commandment)." After this ceremony, they become accountable for their own actions, whereas beforehand they were seen to be under the parents' responsibility for their actions. Additionally, after this time, the individuals are seen as full-fledged members of the Jewish community.

Virtually all cultures have a rite of passage from childhood to adulthood, except our Western society. Many of them are not as pleasant as the Jewish rite of passage.

Ceremonial blessing is important because ceremony brings emotional closure to certain life seasons and ushers in new seasons. This includes marriage. How do you know if you are married? You had a ceremony to mark that milestone, witnessed by others with the signing of a mutual agreement.

A healthy rite of passage for entering manhood or womanhood can help bring the soul to peace with stepping away from emotional childhood identity and being released into adulthood. If the soul is not released into adulthood, it can strive to prove it by way of sexual immorality, gang violence, chemical abuse, joining the army, or attaining corporate success.

> **CEREMONY BRINGS EMOTIONAL CLOSURE TO CERTAIN LIFE SEASONS AND USHERS IN NEW SEASONS.**

One Christian version of a rite of passage is a bar barakah, or "son of the blessing," and bat barakah, or "daughter of the blessing." We have done this for each one of our first five children at age thirteen (and will do so for our youngest when she reaches that age). We have seen tremendous benefits in the lives of each of our children from doing this ceremonial rite of passage. Their faith in God has been strengthened. Their confidence in their identity has been solidified. They walk in moral excellence, being light and standard bearers in their generation.

As their father, John has put the most effort into the bat or bar barakahs we have held for our children. During the two or three months before the ceremony, he would take the child coming up to age thirteen out at least five times on a communicative "date" to discuss various aspects of what it looks like to transition into emotional man- or womanhood. Discussion centred around topics such as their spiritual walk, taking responsibility for growing in their love and relationship with the Lord, honouring the authorities in their lives, and having a fuller expression of adult identity, all while initially still living at home under our authority. Sexual purity and our expectations for how to handle the transition to courtship and marriage is an important discussion point. Even topics such as financial stewardship, tithing, and giving are discussed.

Not only does the father set the gender for the child at conception, but fathers have a role in helping to set children on the path to destiny. Is it any wonder there has been an evil plan to remove fathers from families either through divorce, abandonment, disinterest, or complacency? Proverbs 17:6 says that "Children's children are the crown of old men, and the glory of children is their father."

If there is no father in the picture willing to walk this role for their children, I encourage mothers to do so, or grandfathers, pastors, or spiritual mothers or fathers.

We have spent money on our children's bat and bar barakahs, invited up to two hundred people to attend, ascribed worth to our children in it, given meaningful and symbolic gifts (such as the ring which represents sexual purity until marriage), and empowered them with vision for life, utilizing verbal blessings, prophecy about destiny, and declarations such as "This is my beloved son (or daughter) in whom I am well pleased." We also made a DVD slide show of each of our children's lives to that point—celebrating their growth from babyhood to the present.

For those who have wanted something like this but did not have parents willing or knowledgeable enough to do so, we, as pastors, have led group bar and bat barakahs, coaching parents on how to participate and bless in the midst of such a celebration. There have been those who have not had parents standing with them but have had friends or other support network people to help them "cross the threshold." We have also had those in their twenties and thirties participate in the group ceremonies as they longed for such a blessing, never obtained it, and were seeking the blessing released later in life.

There are five key areas to which we ask our children to commit in this ceremony:

1. To enter into a settled sense of adult identity—into manhood or womanhood (An example of what we would have them say is, "I accept and embrace entering into womanhood from this time forth.)

2. To enter into a clear and settled sense of adult destiny as a follower of Jesus Christ ("I have dedicated my life to serving Jesus Christ.")

3. To take adult responsibility for their own spiritual health from the time of the ceremony ("From this time forth, I will take spiritual responsibility for my own life, all the while receiving counsel from my parents and trusted others.")

4. To honour their parents and authority figures in their life ("I commit to an ongoing relationship with my parents, and to a continued honour of them as God's primary instruments of character growth and development in my life. I commit to honour all legitimate authority in my life, whether it be parental, church, school, or civil.")

5. To walk in emotional and sexual purity all the days of their adult life and to remain sexually pure until marriage ("I commit to relating to members of the opposite sex while single in accordance with the principles of godly friendship and courtship, as opposed to dating. I make a specific commitment to a lifetime of sexual purity, emotional purity, and marital fidelity in covenant.")

In turn, we as parents make commitments to our son or daughter:

1. To love them
2. To pray for them regularly
3. To teach them God's principles for life

4. To continue to honour them with open communication and understanding
5. To be available for counsel
6. To partner in prayer with them regarding God's choice and timing for a marriage partner
7. To continue to apply age-appropriate godly discipline to their lives, as God directs, for character development

An excellence resource on this important ceremonial blessing can be obtained by reading Craig Hill's book, *Bar Barakah*.

A sample order of a bat or bar barakah ceremony can be seen below.

ORDER OF CEREMONY

1. Introduction to the ceremony (father preferably; can be done by mother or pastor)
2. Song (or short worship time)
3. Message on the importance of the rite of passage ceremony, including a charge to adulthood
4. Celebration of the child's life (DVD)
5. Skits (tend to be funny renditions of episodes in their lives)
6. Commitments (parents recite their commitments; child recites his/her commitments)
7. Presentation of gifts, with an explanation of what they represent: sandals or shoes (symbolizing sonship), change of clothes (change of garments symbolizing change of season), a gift according to their prophetic destiny (for example we gave Judah a guitar—he is now a worship leader; we gave Aquila a violin—she is now a violinist), a ring (presented symbolizing sexual purity until marriage and is to be worn on the left-hand ring finger)
8. Communion (taken by father, mother, and child, sealing this agreement in Jesus)
9. Signing of covenant certificate

10. Reading of past prophetic words or giving of prophetic words or blessings (by those significant to the candidate: parent, grandparent, pastor, teacher, mentor, friend)
11. Symbolic expression of womanhood or manhood (all the men or women over the age of thirteen go to one part of the room and then call over the candidate to come join them—as in crossing a threshold)
12. Declaration of womanhood or manhood (by the father or mother, usually including, "This is my beloved son [or daughter] in whom I am well pleased.")
13. Closing prayer and release to celebration (food, fellowship)

A NOTE FROM MY HUSBAND, JOHN BOOTSMA

Having not been privileged as a teen to receive a personal blessing party, navigating the waters of a bar barakah released within me great joy, yet not without sadness. While overjoyed at the realization that I had authority to release my beloved children into a destiny I had never dreamed possible for myself, I also held remorse that my personal capacity to dream and believe had been held back. I attributed this in part to not having been privileged to receive the value in my identity or impartation in my destiny that a rite of passage ceremony was designed to release.

The impact of this gift we were enabled to release to our firstborn impacted me to even greater depths when a precious woman in her sixties, having lived with the crippling effects of rheumatoid arthritis for much of her life, came to speak to me after Judah's bar barakah ceremony. With a level of bittersweetness, she expressed the beauty of what she had just witnessed by saying, "John, I can't imagine how different my life would have been, had my parents done this for me."

Wow Jesus! "The secret things belong to the LORD our God, but those things which are revealed belong to us and to our children forever" *(Deuteronomy 29:29). As a dad who has now conducted five* of our own six children's rite of passage celebrations, plus orchestrated and officiated at two others, I am so grateful to the Lord for unveiling the power of this blessing, this empowerment to prosper ceremony, the loss of which has paved the way for much unnecessary suffering in our Western culture.

NEXT GENERATION TESTIMONIAL

Judah Bootsma, our twenty-three-year-old son
STRATFORD, CANADA

Blessing can so catapult a young boy into a mature young man. Just one way for me was when I turned thirteen, my parents held a big bar barakah party for me at the church. They invited many friends and family and put a lot of time, energy, and money into it. It wasn't weird like I initially thought it could have been.

They really blessed me with gifts and words that all had meaning and purpose. For example, I received a ring to wear to symbolize purity until I met my wife and a guitar to encourage my talent in music. It wasn't a meaningless party, and the blessing and new responsibility I had as a man were not given lightly. Nor did I treat it lightly afterwards. What my parents set out to accomplish really did work. With God's grace, I kept my purity and virginity for marriage, and I was so glad to find my wife had done the same. I learned the guitar and drums. Throughout the years, I have been to a few different music schools, helped in houses of prayer, led worship, and have used and am using the talent that God has given me.

I also put my focus on God through high school and my teenage years—even till now. He has never let me down. I can't say there haven't been hard or dry seasons. However, through it all, I knew where I stood, and with a solid foundation and support, I knew that I could overcome what life would throw at me.

NOTES

1. Terry and Melissa Bone, accessed October 23, 2014,
http://www.powerofblessing.com/_store/_preview/pob_preview.pdf.
2. Ibid.
3. Ibid.
4. Ibid.
5. Ibid.
6. Ibid.

5

THE WORD OF GOD

*And that from childhood you have
known the Holy Scriptures . . .*
2 TIMOTHY 3:15

COUNT NICOLAUS LUDWIG VON ZINZENDORF was six weeks old
when his dying father gave him to the service of Jesus. His mother remarried when he was four years old, and he went to live with
his godly, Pietist grandmother, Henrietta Catharina von Gersdorf.
Zinzendorf was taught the scriptures on a daily basis, memorizing
passages, loving his Bible study times. He said this of himself, "Already in my childhood . . . I loved the Saviour, and had abundant
communion with Him. In my fourth year I began to seek God ear-
nestly, and determined to become a true servant of Jesus Christ . . . A
thousand times I heard Him speak in my heart and saw Him with
the eye of faith."[1] At age six, as he was praying one day, Charles XII's
soldiers broke into the house, bent on destruction. "The lad began
to speak of Christ . . . the soldiers fled in awe and terror."[2]

Count Zinzendorf went on to open his estate as an asylum to
persecuted believers from Moravia and Bohemia where they built
the village of Herrnhut and became known as the Moravians. This
became the birthplace of a 24/7 prayer movement that continued

for 120 years, launching a missions movement that set up missionary colonies in the West Indies, Greenland, among the North American Indians, Suriname, South America, East Indies, Egypt, South Africa and to the Inuit of Labrador.

Count Zinzendorf's life was marked by his grandmother's training in the Word of God. How important it is for us as parents to teach our children to love and study the Word of God. The precious Word of God, handbook for our lives, must be something we impart to this next generation.

"This Book of the Law shall not depart from your mouth, but you shall meditate in it day and night, that you may observe to do according to all that is written in it. For then you will make your way prosperous, and then you will have good success" (Joshua 1:8).

"And that from childhood you have known the Holy Scriptures, which are able to make you wise for salvation through faith which is in Christ Jesus. All Scripture is given by inspiration of God, and is profitable for doctrine, for reproof, for correction, for instruction in righteousness, that the man of God may be complete, thoroughly equipped for every good work" (2 Timothy 3:15–17).

Since we desire for our children to have a prosperous way, have good success, be wise, and be complete and thoroughly equipped for every good work, these scriptures make clear that meditation on and knowledge of the Word of God is paramount.

A habit John and I have exercised with our children is to read a portion of scripture at the breakfast and dinner table as we gather together as a family (or even if it is one of us with what children are there). We read from *The Golden Children's Bible,* which we find very accurate to the original texts. We will then ask questions from the passage to see how sharply everyone was listening! It has proved, over the years, to give our children a solid foundation of biblical

> **THE PRECIOUS WORD OF GOD, HANDBOOK FOR OUR LIVES, MUST BE SOMETHING WE IMPART TO THIS NEXT GENERATION.**

knowledge all the while being an enjoyable family exercise. As soon as each child is able to read, they are given their own Bible and we set a morning devotion time for them that needs to include time in the Word. When they are young, children will need reminding to have their "God time." Yet the daily reminders will pay off in large dividends as they develop a love for the Word and, more importantly, for the Author of the Word.

BEDTIME ROUTINES

Developing a healthy bedtime routine with younger children helps establish strong bonding between parent and child and is a golden opportunity to impart godly values and learn biblical truths. It is amazing what kind of meaningful discussions can stem from those routines. Over the years, John and I have used this time to read books to our children, have heart communication time, and impart scriptural truths. John, in particular, has been diligent to teach our children scripture memorization at bedtime. He will quote a verse and have them repeat it, reinforcing the chosen verse each night until it is committed to memory.

"How can a young man cleanse his way? By taking heed according to Your word. With my whole heart I have sought You; Oh, let me not wander from Your commandments! Your word I have hidden in my heart, that I might not sin against You" (Psalm 119:9–11).

Some of our youngest daughter's favourite books she and her dad have read in the evenings are: *The One Year Father-Daughter Devotions*, by Jesse Florea, Leon C. Wirth, and Bob Smithouser; *Teach It to Your Children: How Kids Lived in Bible Days*, by Miriam Feinberg Vamosh; and *Children's Adoration Prayer Book*, by Bob Hartley.

We have also read together through series such as Laura Ingalls Wilder's Little House and C. S. Lewis' The Chronicles of Narnia. Other favourite books are *Charlotte's Web* by E. B. White, *The Velveteen Rabbit* by Margery Williams, *Children Can You Hear Me: How to Hear and See God* by Brad Jersak, and *Guess How Much I Love You* by Sam McBratney.

As our older children grew, the content of the nighttime routine would change. Yet right up until our son left home to go to college and then later to marry, he would knock on our bedroom door when he came home in the evenings to say good night and give us a hug. For our out-of-the-house older children, we treasure those meaningful nighttime memories. For our younger ones still at home, we are in the midst of still forming them.

FAMILY CELL

John or I will lead a family cell night where we take a short time to worship (often, one of our kids will lead), have an exhortation from the Word, and then pray. We were very diligent in doing this weekly for a period of time then got off schedule, but we are back on track. It is important to keep it short and to keep it interesting, otherwise the children's attention will wander. We have also had the older children lead in the family cell so they are responsible for the teaching times, which has been a rich experience.

Some families have pizza and home-movie night, or popcorn and pajamas board-game night. Setting aside a minimum of one evening a week to do family-oriented activities can be very bonding, not only between parent and child, but also between siblings.

On a cruise-ship vacation with our three oldest children, John and I set a schedule for a daily meeting in the ship's chapel where the five of us took turns leading morning prayer and Bible study. In the midst of the Caribbean and attractions of a five-star cruise ship, my favourite times on that vacation were our morning family devotion times.

HONOURING THE WORD

Wycliffe Bible Translators have indicated there are at least 1,860 dialects or heart languages in the earth that do not have the translated Bible. They are seeking to end this "Bible poverty."[3]

The blood of many martyrs was shed so you and I could have a Bible in our hands in our language. William Tyndale, who in the early sixteenth century translated the scriptures into English, used the newly invented Gutenberg printing press to produce copies to be distributed widely. The price he paid to do so was execution by strangulation, with his body burned at the stake. I remember standing on the banks of the River Thames in London, where I was told the first smuggled Tyndale Bibles were brought to England. I was moved by that place of history where the English Word of God came to the everyday believer.

The book *Jesus Freaks* tells the story of a Chinese underground church that was raided by police. The congregants were told to spit on a Bible that had been thrown on the floor, and if they did so, they would be allowed to leave. Starting with the pastor, one by one, they spit on the Bible and exited the room. That is, until a quiet sixteen-year-old came forward, wiped the spit off the Bible with her dress, and repented for how the others had denied and dishonoured the Word. A gun was placed to her head. The trigger was pulled. She went on to a reward in heaven for standing for truth.[4] But what would you or I do if we were in that scenario?

I was twenty years old and on a hovercraft from Hong Kong with Bibles hidden in my clothes and bag. Along with others on the team, led by Jackie Pullinger, we had five hundred Chinese-print Bibles we were hoping to smuggle into mainland China. I was detained at the border by two angry guards who put the Chinese Bible in my face and asked me to read it. As the commotion was going on with me, my team members quietly slipped behind me through the border checkpoint. Surprisingly, after one guard went to another room, the lone guard left put my Bibles back in my bag, instructing me harshly to go. Our handoff of the Bibles to the underground believers was all done at night in secret. That experience marked me with the preciousness of the Word of God. These believers were putting their freedom, indeed their lives, in danger for possessing this book. Yet, they were so eager not only to obtain but also to read, study, and devour the Bible.

Are we honouring, studying, and hiding in our hearts this precious Word given to us? Paul admonishes Timothy in First Timothy 4:13 to give attention to reading, but in Second Timothy 2:15 he emphasizes studying like a worker: "Be diligent to present yourself approved to God, a worker who does not need to be ashamed, rightly dividing the word of truth." Correct application of God's Word is the result of diligent study. If believers took stock of how much time they actually spent in reading and studying the Word of God, most would be shocked at how little time they invest in such an important tool for Christian growth and maturity. Simple yet profound is the principle of diligence in the daily, and it is easier to learn that diligence at a young age.

Developing a Bible study plan in our life is important for growth in God. I prefer to read a passage from the Old Testament and a passage from the New Testament each day, thereby continuously reading through the Bible simultaneously in both Testaments. I believe if we leave out reading and studying the Old Testament we are greatly handicapped when it comes to understanding the plan of redemption the Father wove all through history to bring us into relationship with Him. Greater wisdom comes each time we reread a passage. We gain insight we did not grasp before as we reread and study passages, asking the Holy Spirit to illuminate the truths therein. Teaching our children to read through passages and not just skip here and there will help.

In the summer of 2008, the Lord spoke clearly to me to take our family to the Onething conference coming up in December in Kansas City, held by the International House of Prayer. It is a young-adult conference, but since the Lord made these instructions so clear, we packed up our whole family and headed on an eighteen-hour drive to Kansas City two days after Christmas. It was a divine appointment. Mike Bickle's teaching emphasis that year was on eschatology. The conference ended with a call to a commitment to radical pursuit of God, called the Sacred Charge. The seven commitments thousands made that night were to pray daily, fast weekly, do justly (acts of justice), give extravagantly, live holy, lead diligently, and speak boldly. The pray-daily commitment included pray-reading the scriptures daily and diligent study. Specifically that night, a commitment was made to study the book of Revelation for the next three years. John and I and our three oldest children, Judah, seventeen at that time; Gabrielle, fifteen; and Aquila, aged thirteen, took that charge and commitment, and all of us studied Revelation diligently the next three years, as well as the other 150 biblical chapters that relate to the end times. There were many times when we studied together and quizzed each other on our scriptural knowledge.

Utilizing Bible commentaries can be helpful in Bible study. For the book of Revelation, an excellent resource is Mike Bickle's *Book of Revelation Study Guide*. Some good online resources include biblegateway.com for a free concordance, soniclight.com for Dr. Thomas Constable's *Expository Bible Study Notes* for each of the books of the Bible, mikebickle.org for a teaching library, and cbn.com where you can sign up to receive daily emails with the portion of scripture to read and study each day in order to go through the Bible in a year. My husband purchased an online program called Accordance for me, which is a very helpful tool in Bible study. It has Hebrew, Greek, commentaries, maps, concordances, and other tools helpful to gain greater biblical insight.

Richard J. Foster begins his classic book *Celebration of Discipline: The Path to Spiritual Growth* with this statement, "Superficiality is the curse of our age. The doctrine of instant satisfaction is a primary spiritual problem. The desperate need today is not for a greater number of intelligent people, or gifted people, but for deep people."[5] Depth of revelation in the Word of God comes through time spent reading, studying, and meditating on the truths within. May we, and our children, be gripped with a love for the scriptures and Holy-Spirit-inspired understanding.

PRAYING THE WORD

"'As for Me', says the LORD, 'this is My covenant with them: My Spirit who is upon you, and My words which I have put in your mouth, shall not depart from your mouth, nor from the mouth of your descendants, nor from the mouth of your descendants' descendants', says the LORD, 'from this time and forevermore'" (Isaiah 59:21).

According to *The Spirit-Filled Life Bible,* a Hebrew word for meditate is *hagah,* meaning to reflect, to mutter, to ponder, or to contemplate while repeating something aloud. "In Hebrew thought, to meditate upon the Scriptures is to quietly repeat them in a soft, droning sound, while utterly abandoning outside distractions. From this tradition comes a specialized type of Jewish prayer called 'davening', that is, reciting texts, praying intense prayers, or getting lost in communion with God while bowing or rocking back and forth. Evidently, this dynamic form of meditation/prayer goes back to David's time."[6] If you have seen pictures of Jewish mediation at the Western (Wailing) Wall, you will understand what this looks like.

Although I am not saying children need to rock back and forth, the meditative component of pray-reading and repeating the scriptures out loud will help them retain what they are reading and connect to the living Word—Jesus. If a particular verse admonishes us to obey, we can turn it into a declaration such as, "I set my heart to obey You in this directive. Strengthen me to heed Your words and build my life on the rock of Your commands (Matthew 7:24–29)." If a passage expresses a truth we are to believe, we can thank God for this truth and ask Him to reveal more of His heart to us as it pertains to that truth. Turn the Word into meditative dialogue with the Author.

Speaking to the Jews in John 5:39–40, Jesus said, "You search the Scriptures, for in them you think you have eternal life; and these are they which testify of Me. But you are not willing to come to Me that you may have life." Notice Jesus is saying the words and letters of the scriptures themselves do not contain life but it is the written Word leading us to the living Word—Jesus Himself—that produces life. We can come to Him, access Him, through Spirit-inspired meditation on His Word. And we can teach our children to do the same.

TURN THE WORD INTO MEDITATIVE DIALOGUE WITH THE AUTHOR.

Our daughter Gabrielle's love for the Word of God was evident before she became a teenager. She was leading an end-times study group at age fifteen that adults up to the age of sixty-five attended. Presently, at age twenty-one, her knowledge of the Word of God astounds me.

She has recently graduated from the International House of Prayer University in Kansas City with a degree in theology and a major in house of prayer leadership. From reading the children's Bible at the dinner table, bedtime scripture memorization, and the initially forced Bible study times as a young child, Gabrielle's heart has been gripped by a love for the Word and for the beauty of the Author of the Word.

"Your word is a lamp to my feet and a light to my path" (Psalm 119:105).

NEXT GENERATION TESTIMONIALS

Glory Anna Bootsma, our eleven-year-old daughter

My dad reads to me every night from books, and he helps me memorize scripture. Because my dad is gone to work during the day, when he reads to me at night it helps me feel close to him and know how much he loves me.

Memorizing the Bible has helped me know what God has to say about my life and how much I am loved. I say those verses in my head often as I go through the day.

Benjamin Nunez, twenty-eight-year-old staff leader at the International House of Prayer of Kansas City
ORIGINALLY FROM CUERNAVACA, MEXICO

As I grew up, I started working in different expressions of ministry, like evangelism and children's ministry. From thirteen to seventeen years old, I would go almost every weekend with my friends to the streets, hospitals, and parks to preach the gospel. We would see the power and mercy of God operating through us. But I remember how I felt a failure in my secret life of prayer, and it was true. I used to view prayer as the "price we pay" if we wanted power and success in ministry, the "means" to get anointing. I knew something had to change, because I got to the point when I realized that I was hitting a wall in my life, and I needed reality; I needed joy in His presence. I knew there was something greater than miracles, a successful ministry, and the excitement of missions. Little did I know that God was about to change my life radically.

At the age of seventeen, I decided to take a year off to find God before I went to college. During this time, God encountered me one day and told me, "Build Me a house of prayer, like David did, and be the first one to be there." This word changed my life, because I received a hunger for prayer. But I knew none who would give me answers about this house of prayer, until someone gave me a book named "Passion for Jesus," by Mike Bickle. When I read it, I couldn't stop crying in my bedroom. I knew that I had found a spiritual father, and I wanted his DNA. So I decided to study English just to be able to translate all his material for myself and for others around me. I just wanted all my friends to know this reality.

Little did I know that this journey into prayer was actually a journey of studying the Bible in a deeper way. Without realizing, after two years, my thirst for prayer increased due to studying so many writings of Mike's. He became my "long-distance spiritual father." I remember listening to at least two teachings a day and taking notes in

Spanish, then praying with that. My notes would become my prayer language. Then I realized that the Word was actually the beginning of any prayer.

Mike has been key in my life. Now that I work with him in Kansas City, I realize that his life of prayer is greater than his writings about prayer. His life provokes me all the time to be faithful in the place of prayer and to study the Word for real. He always encourages me to lose my twenties, thirties, and forties in the place of prayer and study of the Word and to have a real history in God, so then in my fifties, sixties, and seventies I can have a message that will change the earth with the living Word of God. He was the first leader to encourage me to not focus on success in ministry, but on the reality that happens in my heart when I close my eyes and talk to Jesus.

NOTES

1. J. E. Hutton, *A History of the Moravian Church*, 2nd ed.,1909, accessed October 23, 2014, http://www.ccel.org/ccel/hutton/moravian.v.i.html
2. Ibid.
3. *Wycliffe Global Alliance*, "Scripture & Language Statistics 2013," accessed October 23, 2014, http://www.wycliffe.net/resources/scriptureaccessstatistics/tabid/99/Default.aspx
4. DC Talk and Voice of the Martyrs, *Jesus Freaks* (Tulsa, OK: Albury Publishing, 1999), 50–51.
5. Richard J. Foster, *Celebration of Discipline: The Path to Spiritual Growth* (New York: HarperCollins, 1988), 1.
6. *Spirit-Filled Life Bible, NKJV*, Jack W. Hayford, General Editor (Nashville: Thomas Nelson Publishers, 1991), 753–754.

6

THE REVELATORY GIFT

Your sons and your daughters shall prophesy.
JOEL 2:28

JOHN AND I HAVE LEANED heavily on hearing the voice of God and receiving His wisdom and direction in raising our children. Since He is the best Father, His wisdom in parenting is incalculably helpful.

First Corinthians 14:1 says, "Pursue love, and desire spiritual gifts, but especially that you may prophesy." The word *desire* is used to describe how we are to long for spiritual gifts, especially prophecy. The Greek word for *desire* is *zeloo*. It means "to be zealous for, to burn with desire, to pursue ardently, and to desire eagerly or intensely."[1] It is in this passionate manner you and I, our children, and those we mentor, are divinely instructed to go after the prophetic gift. It is indeed a gift given from heaven, but it also is something we develop. How wonderful to begin to develop the gift as a child. In fact, children are born with a sensitivity to the spirit realm. For example, I have noticed it is quite common for small children raised in Christian homes to see angels. If we are careful to protect and foster that sensitivity to the Lord, His words, and His presence, it helps develop a life-long journey of walking closely with the Saviour.

As a child I had a revelatory gift, but I was ignorant as to how to use it, and I often saw the demonic side. I literally would see things in my bedroom with my natural eyes and not just my spiritual eyes. Scary images, figures like puppets, would move about my room. Even hearing audible scary voices was occasionally a part of my night life. I needed to learn how to pray away the dark side and develop the revelatory gift as it pertained to what God was saying and doing.

I literally learned to ride a pony before I could walk, and there are pictures of me riding at six months old—with some assistance, of course, at that point! By age four and five I would ride my pony in the fields and talk to God. I would listen, and somehow I felt Him speak to me in the sky, the wind, the birds, the fields. At age eight I had an encounter that changed my life.

I was visited by two individuals who prophesied over my life. They told me I would travel the world, preach, lead many to Jesus, and be a part of revival. Although at that age I couldn't comprehend all that was spoken, my heart burned within me. I can't prove it, but I have suspected they were angels that came in human form (Hebrews 13:2). As mentioned earlier, I was not born again until age twelve, yet as a small child I was marked by God.

I believe all children are marked by God in some way. It is the fostering, the developing, the responsiveness to and maturing of that call that takes us into destiny.

HEARING THE VOICE OF GOD

Jesus stated in John 10:27, "My sheep hear My voice, and I know them, and they follow Me."

Psalm 40:5 states, "Your thoughts toward us cannot be recounted to You in order; if I would declare and speak of them, they are more than can be numbered." Similarly, Psalm 139:17–18 says, "How precious also are Your thoughts to me, O God! How great is the sum of them! If I should count them, they would be more in number than the sand." God's thoughts towards us are more numerous than the grains of sand on the seashore. That is astounding! Many times I have walked a beach and thought of this passage. Imagine a desert and how much sand is in it. One handful alone is said to contain approximately ten thousand grains. Yet God's thoughts towards you outnumber the sand. When we endeavour to hear His voice, we simply tap into those thoughts. There is never a shortage of His thoughts towards you. We never have to convince God to speak to us. He is an extremely communicative Father.

ALL CHILDREN ARE MARKED BY GOD IN SOME WAY. IT IS THE FOSTERING, THE DEVELOPING, THE RESPONSIVENESS TO AND MATURING OF THAT CALL THAT TAKES US INTO DESTINY.

Jeremiah 29:11–13 tells us the nature of these thoughts: "For I know the thoughts that I think toward you, says the LORD, thoughts of peace and not of evil, to give you a future and a hope. Then you will call upon Me and go and pray to Me, and I will listen to you. And you will seek Me and find Me, when you search for Me with all your heart."

Part of the role of the Holy Spirit is to speak to us. Jesus is speaking in John 16:12–15: "I still have many things to say to you, but you cannot bear them now. However, when He, the Spirit of truth, has come, He will guide you into all truth; for He will not speak on His own authority, but whatever He hears He will speak; and He will tell you things to come. He will glorify Me, for He will take of what is Mine and declare it to you. All things that the Father has are Mine. Therefore I said that He will take of Mine and declare it to you." The Holy Spirit represents the Father and Son consistently. When we seek to "hear" from this supernatural realm, we do not listen outwardly but rather inwardly.

Mark Virkler, an American Baptist pastor, took a year out of his life to learn to hear the voice of God. Mark developed the following four simple keys to hear God's voice, from Habakkuk 2:1–2. "I will stand my watch and set myself on the rampart, and watch to see what He will say to me, and what I will answer when I am corrected. Then the LORD answered me and said: 'Write the vision . . .'"

Key #1. *Become still so you can sense God's flow of thoughts and emotions within.* "I will stand my watch" (on my guard post). Dialing down the busyness of our minds and our lives helps us tune in to the sweet stillness of the Spirit's presence.

Key #2. *As you pray, fix the eyes of your heart upon Jesus.* "I will . . . watch to see what He will say to me." Turning our inner attention to the Lord, opening the eyes of our heart or understanding, awakens the divine flow from within. Ephesians 1:18 speaks of the "eyes of your understanding [heart] being enlightened." King David used the eyes of his heart to picture the Lord at his right hand (Psalm 16:8; Acts 2:25). This is an example we can follow.

Key #3. *God's voice in your heart often sounds like a flow of spontaneous thoughts.* Where we may be expecting God to speak to us in an audible voice or booming inner channel, more often He speaks in spontaneous thoughts, visions, feelings, or impressions. Tune into those spontaneous God thoughts.

Key #4. *Journaling, that is, the writing out of your prayers and God's answers, brings great freedom in hearing God's voice.* Habakkuk 2:2 "Then the LORD answered me and said: 'Write [record] the vision . . .'" Recording helps us tap into a flow of the spontaneous words and vision of God. Testing the words later to ensure they align with scripture and the character and nature of God is necessary.[2]

With each of my children I have taken these four principles and, explaining them in a language appropriate to their age, have taught them that they too can hear the voice of God. As a part of their daily time with God, we have instructed our children to journal, or hear the Lord and write out what He is saying.

When our children are younger, we remind them to have their time with the Lord and to journal. We do not start homeschooling activities until their personal time with the Lord is completed. As our older children grew, this daily discipline was already instilled in them, so now they hear God's voice and journal every day as a part of their life. Just this week I was sitting in the house of prayer next to both of my older daughters. I noticed them listening to the Lord and writing out the revelation they received in their journals. As a mother, it was a delight to my heart to see them communing with their heavenly Father.

This next generation is very attuned to the spirit realm. Many are seekers of spiritual experiences but tend to look for it in the occult, tarot card readers, fortune tellers, psychics, and godless meditation or séances. There is a need to reveal the true functioning of the prophetic to this generation. One of the best ways to learn to live a prophetic life is to exercise hearing the voice of God on a daily basis. So many are just longing to be taught how to do this.

JUDGING THE WORDS

Scripture teaches us to judge the prophetic. As you train your children or those you mentor in hearing God's voice, make judging the word a part of their equipping. Whatever is of the Lord will pass His tests. Here are some basic tests to determine whether what we and our children hear from the revelatory realm is from God:

1. Prophetic words that are truly from God will align with and be consistent with the written Word of God.
2. The Lord's words will be according to His nature of love, since God is love (1 John 4:8).
3. Since it is the Holy Spirit who speaks to us, His words will be filled with the fruit of the Spirit: love, joy, peace, patience, kindness, goodness, faithfulness, gentleness, and self-control (Galatians 5:22–23). Anything we hear that makes us nervous,

anxious, or lacking peace can be judged as not from the Spirit of God.

4. All true words from the Lord will be consistent with the testimony of Jesus (His witness, His words) as Revelation 19:10 declares.

5. The Father's words will also be in some way edifying, exhorting, and comforting as First Corinthians 14:3 admonishes. Even when we are corrected or confronted to come higher in character and deeds, it will give us hope and take us ultimately to a place of edification.

6. God's words will receive confirmation from other mature believers who hear the voice of God.

7. Does it come to pass? If we, those we mentor, or our children hear anything directional, check to see if it materializes. Tracking our accuracy helps us recognize His voice in the future.

WAYS TO RECEIVE PROPHETIC REVELATION

As we teach our children the many ways God imparts revelation, it helps them to realize His revelation can come in varying forms:

1. *The Word.* The scriptures are the most important way we hear God speak.

2. *Still, small voice.* In an interaction with Elijah, God was not in the wind, earthquake, or fire, but in a still, small, voice (1 Kings 19:11–12). Often this voice can sound like our own thoughts as the Lord communicates to us subtly as His thoughts invade ours.

3. *Visions and pictures.* Paul's prayer of Ephesians 1 includes a petition for the eyes of our understanding (or heart) to be enlightened. Jesus said this of Himself, "Most assuredly, I say to you, the Son can do nothing of Himself, but what He sees the Father do; for whatever He does, the Son also does in like manner" (John 5:19). Encourage your child to pay attention to visions or prophetic pictures that come to them, particularly as

they ask for them and position themselves to receive. We will sometimes exercise the prophetic together as a family, particularly if we need direction. We will all wait on the Lord, listen, and pay attention to the thoughts or pictures or visions that come. For example, this family exercise has been most helpful in discerning where to go on vacation.

4. *Dreams.* Although not all dreams we have will be from God, as they are the natural processing of information in our minds that occurs at night, this is still an important way the Lord speaks to His people. We have taught our children to honour their dreams. This can include sharing them with us as their parents, writing them out, praying into them, dialoguing with God about them, and obeying instruction given in them. It was in a dream the Lord appeared to Solomon to ask him what he desired (1 Kings 3:5); it was through dreams an angel appeared to tell Joseph first to take Mary as his wife (Matthew 1:20), later to flee to Egypt (Matthew 2:13), to come back to Israel when danger had passed (vv. 19–20), and specifically to go to the region of Galilee (v. 22). We can experience warnings in dreams, often for the purpose of intercession to interrupt any evil plans and instead invite the kingdom of God to invade a specific situation.

When Aquila was six years of age, she came to me at breakfast time, stating she'd had a disturbing dream in which her younger sister Phoebe fell and hurt herself badly. We prayed against any dark plans, asked God to protect Phoebe, and went on with our day. That afternoon, I had put our four-year-old (and developmentally delayed) Phoebe in her third-story bedroom for a nap. The window was open but the screen was on the window. When a neighbour frantically knocked on our door telling us to go to Phoebe, I ran to her room to find she had somehow removed the screen and was hanging on the windowsill about to fall. I pulled her from the window in the nick of time. Then I remembered Aquila's dream. It is possible that if we had ignored Aquila's dream and not prayed against any negative plans, things could have turned out differently that day.

5. *Word of Knowledge.* A word of knowledge is simply insight or information given divinely (1 Corinthians 12:8).

6. *Word of Wisdom.* When the Lord gives divine instruction, blueprints, or insight into certain situations, it can be called a word of wisdom (1 Corinthians 12:8). As we ask for wisdom in life circumstances, we will receive it.

7. *Discernment.* Also referred to as impressions, discernment is the ability to differentiate what is of God and what is not (1 Corinthians 12:10). Especially as the Evil One parades himself as an angel of light, discernment is needed so that we do not participate in things that are not pleasing to the Lord. I have found my discernment helpful in such things as knowing which movies are okay for my children to watch and which are not okay. A check in my spirit will indicate what movie is not acceptable—often from just hearing its title or looking at the trailer for it. We need to pay attention to our impressions (gut instinct). As we become more and more sanctified and wholly given to the Lord, our impressions and discernment will increase in accuracy.

8. *Peace or lack of peace.* Since peace is one of the fruits of the Spirit (Galatians 5:22), the Spirit will use peace as a way to communicate to us. Particularly for decisions that need to be made, teach your child to pay attention to what level of peace they have.

9. *Circumstances.* Doors that open and doors that close can be indications of God's will. If we are banging on doors that simply refuse to budge, it isn't always the devil holding it closed. It may not be the best for your child, or the timing may not be right. When the disciples would come to a city that refused them, they were instructed to shake the dust off their feet and go else-

where (Matthew 10:14). When Paul found himself shipwrecked on the island of Malta, it only opened up an opportunity to bring the gospel of salvation and healing to that land (Acts 28).

10. *Things in the natural that speak of the supernatural.* Nature itself speaks of God and His handiwork (Psalm 19:1). How can one deny the existence of God when one sees the multitudes of stars, the complexity of the human anatomy, or the beauty of a sunset? Additionally, the Lord can use seemingly ordinary things to speak to us—like a newspaper heading, a billboard, or a particular object that crosses our path at a specific moment in time. John and I were once driving on country roads while discussing our children's department in the church we pastored. We realized the department needed help and we were discussing if we should take turns leading kids ministry or, if not, what should be done. At that moment we came upon a car in front of us with the license plate ACTZ 636. Immediately we said to one another, "Acts 6:3–6, I wonder what that says?" I got out my Bible to read how the apostles were faced with a need for practical help in the ministry. They decided it wise to seek out others to lead this department and they said, "But we will give ourselves continually to prayer and to the ministry of the word." It goes on to say how they chose Stephen and six others and laid hands on them to commission them. Amazingly, a couple months after this incident the Lord gave us a man named Stephen to lead our children's ministry.

11. *Others.* The Lord certainly uses other people to speak to us. They may be giving us a prophecy (1 Corinthians 14) or they may simply be telling a story or speaking to us in a casual setting, but something they say resonates within us as being a word from the Lord. Preachers and teachers certainly communicate to us from the Lord, as well as our children. When our daughter Zoe was six years old she scribbled a note to my husband, "Dad, I want you to come home." It struck him powerfully that

he was too busy and needed to prioritize his time at home with the family.

12. *Angels.* Biblical precedence for angelic activity is large in scope and amount. Angels deliver messages (Daniel 9:21–22), war with the demonic (Daniel 10:13), protect (Psalm 91:11–12), bring freedom (Acts 5:19), minister to God's people (Hebrews 1:14), worship the Lord, and do His bidding (Psalm 103:20–21).

13. *Audible voice of God.* The Lord spoke audibly numerous times in the Bible. As previously mentioned, a significant interaction occurred at Jesus' baptism when the Father affirmed His Son, "You are My beloved Son; in You I am well pleased" (Luke 3:22). My grandmother was in great pain with arthritis for years. She was praying on her knees for others as she did daily when she heard the audible, booming voice of God say, "Pray for yourself." So stunned and used to praying for everyone else, it took the same message to come three times before my grandmother did pray for herself, and she was instantly healed of all arthritis for the rest of her life.

WHAT DOES GOD SAY ABOUT THAT?

Life is filled with questions, decisions, thoughts, hopes, and dreams. Tuning into divine revelation for us, our children, and the lives of those we are mentoring, is immensely helpful in developing relationship with Him, and also for receiving direction in life. Knowing what God has to say about a situation, person, or decision will enable us to maneuver through life, staying on track with His plan for us. God cares about all the big and little things we deal with. He longs to be intimately involved in our lives. From deciding what musical instrument to learn to what person to marry, God has the answers. As we inquire of the Lord on behalf of our children and teach them to inquire on behalf of themselves, we come to divinely led direction, leading to abundance in life. Let's listen to the voice and leadership of Holy Spirit, and teach our children and those we mentor to do the same.

NEXT GENERATION TESTIMONIALS

Aquila Bootsma, our nineteen-year-old daughter
KANSAS CITY, MO

My own testimony with hearing the voice of God begins at a young age when I was first introduced to Communion With God, *by Mark Virkler, as a part of my homeschool curriculum. During those crucial years I learned how hearing God is not as mysterious or remote as we can often think it to be, but that it truly is for the simple and childlike. Jesus said that His sheep hear His voice, and there are no exceptions or "black sheep" in the flock of our Shepherd. There is no better time than now for your children to begin knocking on the door of heaven and hearing the voice of their beloved Father, who is always speaking His words of love over their hearts, and what a privilege it is for you as parents to be a part of bringing them into this reality! The importance of hearing the voice of God is not something that can be overstated. It truly will change your life if you let it.*

I began journaling as soon as I could write. Nearly every morning my parents would wake me up with soft music, and using a paper and pen I would start my day with Him. Something simple that I have seen over the years is the importance of making room for intimacy, taking the time to talk to Him and hear from Him. It's the abiding in love that Jesus talks about in John 15 (one of my favourite sermons in the Bible). Abiding is found in that place of unhindered communion, constant conversation with Him. It is so much simpler and more tangible than we may imagine.

Just a small word of encouragement to all of the parents out there who are in the midst of teaching your children how to hear the voice of God—don't give up! I can honestly say with such gratitude in my heart that this is one of the things from my parents that has had the greatest impact on my life, and it can be the same for your children, too.

Iain McDermid, twenty-seven years old
ENGLAND

I was first taught on hearing the voice of God while I was interning at a church in Oxford, England, in 2010. We had been told that a woman was coming from Canada who had an international prophetic gift, and we would each have time with her for her to pray over us and speak into our lives.

I had heard of the gift of prophecy before and believed that God spoke today, but Patricia Bootsma taught it to us in a way that showed us its practicality, and how it is applicable to everyday life. She revealed through scripture how important it is to take the time to ask God what is on His heart, what He wants to say to us, and what He wants to say to others we meet.

I approached her on the last day for some feedback from a time of worship I had led earlier in the day. Her response changed my life: "It was great; I think you should come to Canada." She talked very briefly about being able to organize visas, gave me her email, and left. I was a little overwhelmed, to say the least. I found out from her that on the first day she had walked into the room (fresh off the plane from Canada) God had highlighted me to her and told her to ask me to come to Canada. It is one thing to hear a word from God, but it is another thing to act on it and walk it out, trusting that it is from God. Through prayer I came to the conclusion that this was a word from God, and it was His plan for me to move to Canada and intern with Patricia. It proved to be one of the best decisions of my life.

It was the most incredible and life-changing experience to serve as an intern at the Catch the Fire Toronto House of Prayer. I was responsible for the musicians and singers and soon became the assistant director to Patricia. I had the privilege of ministering alongside her and many other incredibly talented and gifted people. I made life-long friendships. After a year of serving as Patricia's intern we started working towards the plan for me to stay full-time in the church and lead the house of prayer worship teams in a paid position. For me this was a dream come true . . . and then God spoke to me.

I was over halfway through my second year in Toronto with two months left on my visa when God spoke very clearly that He had other plans for His house of prayer there. God spoke to me through a couple of words from others and then very clearly one evening while I was singing in the house of prayer. He said, "I am going to remove your voice from this house of prayer. In order for you to reach your potential you need to leave here, and in order for the house of prayer to reach its potential, you have to leave." I was so struck by this word that for the remainder of the set I was on my knees, unable to say a word, let alone sing. Patricia had been working so hard with the leadership of the church to create a job for me, and I was being asked by God to give it up and leave. I knew in my heart that God had spoken, and it was now on me to decide if I was going to trust Him or not. I approached Patricia (after much prayer and fasting) and shared with her this word God had given me. We were both deeply saddened, but Patricia trusted that I had heard accurately from God and graciously laid down the position.

If there is one thing that Patricia taught me it is the importance of learning to hear from God yourself. He is always ready to speak with you and share His heart with you, if only we will learn to hear His voice and take the time to listen. God will never set you up to fail, and He is faithful to His word. I moved back to England, and for six months God said I should wait and be ready. Then, seemingly out of nowhere, I received a job offer to become the worship and young adults pastor of Catch the Fire Sydney, Australia! Listening to God, trusting Him, and following His plan is the most exciting and fulfilling experience ever.

NOTES

1. *Spirit-Filled Life Bible, NKJV,* Jack W. Hayford, General Editor (Nashville: Thomas Nelson Publishers, 1991), 1740.

2. Mark and Patti Virkler, *4 Keys to Hearing God's Voice* (Shippensburg, PA: Destiny Image Publishers, Inc., 2010), 2–3. Keys and descriptions used with permission. For more information on this book as well as additional resources, visit Mark and Patti's website, http://www.cwgministries.org/Four-Keys-to-Hearing-Gods-Voice.

7

CULTIVATING A CULTURE OF WORSHIP AND PRAYER

"For I will pour water on him who is thirsty, and floods on the dry ground; I will pour My Spirit on your descendants, and My blessing on your offspring; they will spring up among the grass like willows by the watercourses."
Isaiah 44:3–4

In seeking to foster hearts of passion for the Bridegroom in our children and those we mentor, it is imperative to cultivate in them a value for the culture of worship and prayer both in their private and corporate lives. Adoration and agreement with who God is—through worship—and agreement with what He wants to do in our lives and on the earth—through intercession—are key components in the life of a vibrant believer.

As mentioned in chapter 1, modeling is crucial to multiplication. Being people of prayer and worship ourselves fosters children with the same heart. When they see us giving ourselves persistently to meeting God in the secret and corporate place, it fuels the desire in them.

When our children began to speak—even if they had only mastered a few words—John and I would have them pray after us. We may say, "Thank You, Jesus," or "I love You, Jesus." The repeating of such simple prayers helps jump-start a life of prayer in our toddlers. They will begin to realize they can talk to God just like they talk to us.

In the bedtime routine, there should always be room for prayer. I never really liked the "Now I lay me down to sleep" prayer, since it mentioned potential death before the morning. However, taking turns between adult and child in praying a simple nighttime prayer of consecration, adoration, and intercession is a great way to end a day. When I was a child, I remember always praying for the missionaries around the world before falling asleep. Our eleven-year-old daughter asks her dad to pray with her repeatedly before bed. She doesn't just like one prayer but lots of them!

Around the table before meals, prayers of thanksgiving can be alternated between family members. We also like to hold hands as a family when we pray before a meal. We even do this in restaurants! It feels like we are connected as a family and connecting to a very real God to whom we are grateful for all He has done in giving us daily provision. Prayer around the table is an excellent way for young children to learn to pray out loud in front of others.

In the family cell or time of worship and Bible study we do together, usually weekly, again our children are asked to take turns praying. There is a power in praying as a family that helps unlock destiny. We have prayed together for vehicles, houses, vacation, current affairs around the world, government, grandparents and friends, and seen answered prayer after answered prayer.

It was Ruth Bell Graham who said her morning prayers were directed by the events reported in the daily newspaper. Children learning to pray over conflict in the Middle East or for rain in a drought-stricken area, learn to care for things outside of themselves and their little world.

As our children reached the age of reading independently, they were all given their own full-sized Bible and instructed on having their personal prayer and Bible study. When our eleven-year-old wakes up in the morning, I remind her to have her time with the Lord before she has her breakfast. I don't need to remind our fourteen-year-old, who has already formed the habit.

We have taught them to have, in this personal time, a portion of time set to soak or just be in the presence of God. To foster this, sometimes we will awaken our daughters by playing soft Christian music. Other times, our youngest daughter will join her dad or me in our own soaking time. John has instrumental Christian music playing on his iPad, and he lies on the floor just to abide in the presence of God. Glory Anna sometimes joins him. I have an iPod I play each morning with Spirit-filled instrumental music. It is as though I am getting a wonderful download of the fruit of the Spirit each day—love, joy, peace, patience, goodness, faithfulness, gentleness, and self-control. Glory Anna sometimes takes one of my ear buds and puts it in her ear.

In addition to soaking in His presence, we have taught our children to include prayer time, journaling time (hearing God's voice), and Bible study/reading time in their personal time with God. They are reminded to do this daily as they awake, until the habit is formed, and it is automatically what they do each morning without prompting.

We have taught our children to pray the Bible—taking passages and turning them into dialogue with the Author. Jesus said to the Pharisees in John 5:39–40, "You search the Scriptures, for in them you think you have eternal life; and these are they which testify of Me. But you are not willing to come to Me that you may have life." He was admonishing them to come through the scriptures to the God who authored the scriptures, and not search for life in the words on a page instead of in God Himself. Similarly, we have taught our children to pray the Bible, to make it personal and intimate with the One who longs to meet with them.

Mike Bickle, the director of the International House of Prayer, has said it well when he teaches believers to take verses that admonish us to obey, and turn them into declarations such as, "I set my heart to obey You in this directive. Strengthen me to heed Your words and build my life on the rock of Your commands (Matthew 7:24–29)." Similarly, if a passage expresses a truth we are to believe, we can thank God for this truth and ask Him to reveal more of His heart to us as it pertains to that truth.

Once some of our children hit middle-school age, they liked to use a devotional book to help enhance their prayer and personal study time. We found great resources for pre-teens and teenagers in Focus on the Family's online store.

Additionally, once our daughters reached the age of thirteen we sent them to the International House of Prayer's summer Awakening Teen Camp. We have found the strong culture of prayer at IHOPKC helped boost our early teens' prayer life.

> **PRAYER IS TO BE A CONTINUAL DIALOGUE WITH THE ONE WHO NEVER SLUMBERS AND WHO CARES ABOUT ALL THAT PERTAINS TO US, HIS CHILDREN.**

Developing a culture of prayer includes encouraging our children to pray for that teacher who seems overly strict, for the bully at school, or the friend who is not being inclusive. Of course we want to hear their hearts even when it includes the complaints and issues they deal with. However, turning to God together with your child in such moments, before you try to "fix the problem," teaches them a pattern for life of making prayer a part of every day, throughout the day. Now our children will pray for a parking spot at the mall, or to find the right pair of jeans while shopping. As a family, we take turns praying, from oldest to youngest, in the vehicle just as we are embarking on a journey of over an hour's drive. We pray for protection, joy in our hearts, or whatever the Lord prompts each one to pray. We have seen God's blessings on our travels as a result. Prayer is to be a continual dialogue with the One who never slumbers nor sleeps and who cares about all that pertains to us, His children.

In chapter 3 we discussed having prophetic decrees or prayer lists we use to pray/declare over our children. We want them to develop their own prayer list and decrees. One time our daughter was lamenting that she did not have enough friends. I encouraged her to make it a daily decree that the Lord was giving her new, godly friendships. She did so and amazingly, a lovely girl moved near us and befriended our daughter. She made a new friend in the church, as well. I was encouraged one day when I used a bathroom normally used by our daughter Gabrielle to see her prayer decrees written and taped to her bathroom mirror.

Having a home filled with worship—such as Christian CDs playing, or live streaming the International House of Prayer's prayer room via the website (ihopkc.org/prayerroom), or simply singing a song of worship as we go through the day—models a God-centred focus of worship. I often hear one of my children singing a song through the day. I love the sound of voices raised in worship. I believe our vehicles can also be worship rooms as we play music that exalts Jesus as we drive.

My husband and I have been involved in leading houses of prayer since 2003 and presently lead the Catch the Fire Toronto House of Prayer. I additionally travel domestically and internationally helping to launch houses of prayer. However, I cannot *do* a house of prayer until I *am* a house of prayer and my home is a house of prayer. All of our ministry must start within us, then go into our marriages and children, and from there to others.

When the Lord powerfully encountered me years ago, He spoke in a near-audible voice saying I was to "teach and live and do the tabernacle of David." I knew the tabernacle of David **I CANNOT *DO* A HOUSE OF PRAYER UNTIL I AM A HOUSE OF PRAYER AND MY HOME IS A HOUSE OF PRAYER.**

was in the Bible, but I had no idea how that would affect me today. However, my husband and I had been crying out for God to give us strategies to affect our city and see His Glory come in our church, and we were very hungry for more of His presence. Hence, I began to study the tabernacle of David, finding out this man after God's own heart had established a worship and prayer centre, centred around glorifying the Lord in worship and praying for His purposes on earth. Ministry to the Lord in David's tabernacle continued day and night for decades and coincided with Israel's broadest boundaries in history and greatest time of blessing.

Amos 9:11, quoted in Acts 15:15–17, states that in the last days the Lord will rebuild the tabernacle of David—not a tent pitched over the ark of the covenant, but the spirit, values, and principles of worship and prayer as incense raised up, helping lift His name as great among the nations of the earth (Malachi 1:11).

Personally, I want to be in on that! And, I want my children to be in on that! In fact, I can't think of anything more enjoyable than being in the presence of God, worshiping and adoring Him, taking my place as a priest before Him (Ezekiel 44:15–16). He is worth it all!

John and I started by giving our weekday mornings to the Lord in prayer and worship. From there it developed to taking increased prayer and worship times into the church, launching the corporate house of prayer.

Years ago, when I thought of corporate prayer, images of boring, dry prayer meetings with mostly elderly people in a back room came to mind. However, combining prayer with worship makes prayer so much more intimate and enjoyable. Indeed this is heaven's model as Revelation 5:8–10 reveals, with the bowls of incense being filled with the prayers of the saints, and the harp and the prophetic songs released in worship.

Even while very little, we would take our babies and children to the house of prayer to be with us together as we prayed and worshiped. The truth is, small children may lose focus after a while, but we would set a time frame—of thirty minutes or an hour—when they needed to be in the house of prayer, and then they could go to play in the children's ministry area. Since I am also a homeschool mom, my children have done some of their homeschool work while in the house of prayer. They have also participated as singers, musicians, worship leaders, and intercessors in the house of prayer and do so till this day. In addition to their private times of personal devotions, they have been raised with a corporate culture of prayer and worship that has led to matured love for the Lord in their hearts.

Our son Judah is a worship leader and led the house of prayer in Stratford, the city where we used to live and started a house of prayer. Gabrielle is a worship leader and prayer leader in a house of prayer. Aquila is a violinist and prayer leader in a house of prayer. Zoe has just begun as a singer on the worship team, and Glory Anna and Zoe are taking piano and singing lessons to prepare them to minister in prayer and worship before the Lord.

Perhaps you do not live near an established centre of prayer and worship. How about starting one? Even in your own home. Friends from Bath, England, were so gripped with the revelation to increase prayer and worship in their family and city, they started a home-based family house of prayer with their three teenaged and early-twenties children. They take turns singing, worshiping, and praying together as a family early each morning.

Being a house of prayer leader, I work with a lot of next generation singers, musicians, and intercessors. In fact, I'm amazed at how this next generation is hearing the "sound of the Lord" to fast, pray, and worship unlike any other generation before. As the Lord spoke to me about starting houses of prayer, He said, "If you build it, they will come." And come they have. From Australia, Europe, Asia, Africa, North and South America, the Lord has sent us young people giving themselves to persistent prayer and worship. I have witnessed firsthand their hearts become transformed, their passion for Jesus arise, and their knowledge of the Word expand as they study, sing, and pray it.

How do you motivate a young person to spend hours a day in prayer and worship? You can model it, teach it, impart it, pray for it. But the bottom line is, their hearts meeting with God Himself is the motivator. He shows up! His presence is transforming! We should do what we can do, but we can't do what only God can do. We must trust Him to impact the hearts of our children and those we mentor. Truly, He is the reward! Truly, He is raising up a generation of burning hearts!

NEXT GENERATION TESTIMONIALS

Benjamin Nunez, twenty-eight-year-old staff leader at the International House of Prayer of Kansas City
Originally from Cuernavaca, Mexico

I still remember the first day I encountered prayer; I was around five years old. I remember going downstairs early in the morning and seeing my father kneeling in the living room, praying. That picture shocked me. I'd never seen my father in such a vulnerable position and with such tenderness in his voice. I knew there was something going on within my dad that was different. I remember approaching him and seeing the tears in his eyes. He turned to me and explained, "Son, I am praying; this is the most important thing you will do, talking to God." Then we both kneeled and prayed. It was powerful because it opened my dialogue with God for the first time in a conscious way.

I also remember my mom praying with me and my older brother at night. She would come to my brother's bed and pray with him, then to mine and do the same. But she would take the time to process our little lives with us and then guide us in prayer to give thanks to God. I remember sometimes these were the sweetest moments of the day, because I remember feeling the presence of God in my heart.

My dad has been a pastor for more than forty years and has given me an example of a man of prayer. On the other side, my mom has never been in a pulpit ministering, but she has given her life in intercession for us, mentoring us as kids in a real life of prayer. I am so thankful for my parents—my mentors in the early days.

Gabrielle Bootsma, our twenty-one-year-old daughter

From the time I was a little girl up until now, I've been taught by my parents the importance and impact of prayer. From praying for meals, to praying for parking spots, or praying over one another, I've seen the validity of prayer both in the "results" and in the fact that I'm building relationship with my Father in heaven as I speak to Him. Matthew 6:6 has had a great impact on my life, "But you, when you pray, go into your room, and when you have shut your door, pray to your Father who is in the secret place; and your Father who sees in secret will reward you openly." I took this verse quite literally growing up (and still do), but I remember times as a teenager I would go down to my room, shut my door, and without any music I would (quite dramatically) pray to my Father in the secret place. I think back on those times with such delight because I know that's what the Lord feels when He thinks of those times as well. It's from those times that I've continued to build my relationship with the Lord in the secret place, and now when I wake up in the morning I find that I look forward to reading the Word, praying, journaling, and seeing what the Lord has to say to me for that day.

I would also mention how great an impact the house of prayer has had on my life. From the time I was introduced to the house of prayer in a corporate sense, I was hooked. I loved the fact that we got to sing the Word of God as a form of prayer, and could come together for times of enjoyable intercession. I attribute a lot of my scripture memorization, my depth in the Word, and greatest times of revelation in the Word to the house of prayer—not to mention that my singing and instrumental abilities also grew during those times. I also learned endurance in the place of prayer from spending hours every week for most of my teenage years singing and playing to the Lord in a room with only five to ten other people. The house of prayer has been foundational to my life in God and to keeping a hungry heart for Him, and personally I believe the house of prayer is key for teenagers and young adults to develop and sustain burning hearts for the Lord.

8

COURTSHIP, MARRIAGE, AND LETTING GO

Therefore a man shall leave his father and mother and be joined to his wife, and they shall become one flesh.
GENESIS 2:24

IN MANY ASPECTS OF CURRENT culture, there has been an erosion away from a biblical worldview, even within the church. Sadly, statistics tell us the marriages of fifteen to twenty percent of people who regularly go to church still end in divorce.[1] Somehow we have shifted away, as God's people, from an ideal heavenly design for relationship and marriage. We must be committed to helping our children and those we mentor find God's will for their marriage—it will impact their lives more than almost any other decision. Every day of our children's lives, I have prayed for them to marry only whom the Lord has for them.

On the morning of my wedding day I looked outside at the sun, the blue sky, and some clouds. I heard the Lord speak to my spirit that there was rejoicing going on in heaven today as I was about to marry the man the Lord had chosen for me. At first I wondered if I heard correctly. I said to the Lord, "God, I know the Bible speaks of heaven rejoicing when someone comes into salvation (Luke 15:10), but I don't think it speaks of heaven rejoicing at a wedding." Then the Lord answered me, stating salvation is all about entering into destiny—our destiny as His bride. And marriage was about destiny—the destiny, intertwined, of those the Lord called to live out their days together on earth, helping pull each other into the fullness of what our heavenly Father has for them. Whom you marry plays a big part in who you will become in God. Indeed, there is great pleasure amongst the angels and the Trinity over a marriage designed in the will of God.

In my twenty years of ministering I've seen too many young people derailed from their God-given destiny by whom they married. The apostle Paul stated in Second Corinthians 6:14,

> **THERE IS GREAT PLEASURE AMONGST THE ANGELS AND THE TRINITY OVER A MARRIAGE DESIGNED IN THE WILL OF GOD.**

"Do not be unequally yoked together with unbelievers. For what fellowship has righteousness with lawlessness? And what communion has light with darkness?" I believe this admonishment is a clear warning, not only for believers to not marry or date unbelievers, but also to not marry or date those who are not of the same spiritual fervour or maturity.

I've often heard, "Oh, but I love him. God must want me to marry him since I have such strong emotions." Well, let's look at the life of Solomon. He intermarried with those not of the faith. They turned his heart away from God. And he "clung to them in love" (1 Kings 11:1–3).

Love, or the romantic emotions of the heart, is not the only standard or reason to marry. Additionally, dating with the premise of bringing the person to faith in Jesus, or "missionary dating," most often ends with the believer's heart growing away from God.

The decision of whom to marry must not rest alone on feelings of the heart. Much more is needed, such as the clear leading of the Lord; complementary goals in life; the intertwining of destiny; confirmation from parents and authority figures; and the same spiritual vision and values, including ideas about family, finance, sexuality, child-rearing, and more.

MODERN DATING VS. COURTSHIP (BIBLICAL DATING)

The modern concept of dating is very different from what we see scripturally modeled. Biblical relationships (what I will call biblical dating, or courtship) were often initiated by an interested young man, who would request permission from a girl's father to pursue the possibility of a life-long commitment to her. Any pre-marriage relationship was under the oversight of the father, family, or even the church (or synagogue).

Today's form of dating is more about fleeting enjoyment, multiple romances, playing the field, feeling good about oneself next to a handsome suitor, or checking out various partners to see what one really wants. There is little or no oversight by families.

The end goals of modern dating and biblical dating are very different. Modern dating has little intention or commitment to pursue marriage, whereas courtship is about enjoying each other's company with a goal of determining if it is God's will for the other person to be one's future husband or wife.

Since the oversight of a modern dating relationship is generally left to the couple themselves, there are more opportunities to fall into temptation and not walk in purity. There tends to be much time spent alone. Emotional and physical involvement is expected. Intimacy happens before commitment. By contrast, in biblical dating or courtship, time together in groups with family or friends is encouraged, and there is oversight by and accountability to parents or mentors. This helps to set a standard of righteousness in the relationship—avoiding all compromise, including physical involvement. Commitment happens before intimacy.

MY STORY

I wish I knew when I was a teenager and young adult what I know
now. I navigated the waters of dating poorly. I had various dating
relationships, some of which crossed lines of good sense and biblical standards.

In my book *Convergence* I share my story in the context of the
need for healing of the heart and the discovery of our heavenly
Father's love. To give an abbreviated version here, due to unforgiveness towards and judgements against my father, I walked in a love
deficit that caused me to search for love in wrong places. I vowed
I would never marry anyone like my father. Yet as I sought to date
someone who didn't resemble him in any way, I would end up in
relationships with men who were similar to him. It was as if I had
some sort of sign on my head saying, "Attention, all dysfunctional
men—I'm attracted to you." The nice guys who opened the car door
for me, gave me flowers, and sent nice love letters—I wasn't the
least bit interested in them.

One day, in utter frustration at another failed relationship, I
cried out to the Lord, "I'm so sick of dating. I never want to date
again. What is the name of the man you want me to marry?" Shock-
ingly, I heard the near-audible voice of the Lord say into my spirit,
"John." Thinking I might as well press this a little farther, I asked,
"John who?" Again, a reply came, "John Bootsma." Now, at this
time, I had heard there was a fellow who had recently moved to the
city where I lived who had this name. I had never met him. I had no
idea how old he was or any details of any kind. My sincere reply to
God was, "I can't marry a John; my sister married a John," since my
oldest sister had married a man named John. That was that.

A few weeks later, I met John Bootsma at church. He was a
banker and seemed friendly and handsome enough. He pursued a
relationship with me and since I thought I heard God say he was
going to be my husband, I responded. However, early on I noticed
actions that caused adverse feelings to well up inside my unhealed
heart. John opened the car door for me, gave gifts, and treated me

kindly. I had no grid for kindness and tenderness expressed by a man. I was not attracted to him. I pushed him away.

By the mercy of God's timing, my friend and mentor Carol Arnott had discovered the teachings of John and Paula Sandford on healing of the heart. Carol had recently returned from a trip to their ministry centre, citing transforming experiences in her life. Many times the Lord will use the breakthrough gained in the lives of mentors to become the breakthrough in the lives of those they mentor. When we overcome obstacles, we gain authority in that area to help others similarly gain victory. As I saw firsthand the transformation in Carol, I was determined to see change in my life. I signed up for ministry. I was desperate for breakthrough.

Forgiveness towards my father, repentance for how I had judged him (Romans 2:1), prayer to break the fleshly cycles of sowing and reaping in my life (Galatians 6:7–8), repentance for ungodly beliefs (particularly about men), and prayer for freedom from generational sins and curses in my family line and from demonic oppression were all crucial in my heart's emotional healing.

After that season of healing, I truly felt like a new person and was able to look at John with new eyes. In fact, I found myself not only clearly led to marry him, but now my heart was awakened in love for him.

John and I have enjoyed twenty-four years of an amazing marriage. He is a God-given treasure, an incredible companion in this journey of life. John is a man of integrity, character, and passion for the Lord, and is an amazing husband and father. I'm so grateful to the Lord for helping me navigate the waters of relationships. I also have a deep desire to see this next generation navigate well these same waters, avoiding pitfalls and false starts.

I highly recommend taking time to receive healing of the heart. Even for our children, who we think have been well raised, we have made available healing ministry. For those on our team in ministry, our interns, and any who come to us for advice regarding heart issues, we recommend the ministry of Restoring the

...ations as a tool the Lord is powerfully using to set hearts
.... ..estoringyourlife.org).

THE NAZIRITE VOW

Numbers 6:1–21 speaks of the Nazirite vow. In Hebrew, *nazir*
means "one consecrated, devoted." Nazirites were men or women
who made a voluntary commitment to special consecration and
separation to the Lord. Although there were life-long Nazirites
like Samuel, Samson, and John the Baptist, most people took the
vow for a specific period of time.[2] For believers in modern times,
the Nazirite vow is about living a holy life of consecration, separate from the world. It is a voluntary choice to be dedicated completely to God, and abide by certain conditions and restrictions,
for a defined period of time. *Nazirite DNA*, by Lou Engle, is a good
summary of the modern-day Nazirite vow.

Our son Judah took a Nazirite vow for all of his high school
years to be separated and consecrated to the Lord in a special way.
Part of this vow for him meant he would not pursue girls in any
romantic way. He set himself to seek the Lord and only become
romantically attached to the woman God had for him in marriage.
I remember walking down the street one day with our very handsome, six feet six, blonde son when girls passing us stared at him
in admiration. I could detect they were hoping for his attention.
Judah walked on and never even noticed them. I can't say Judah
never noticed *any* pretty girls in all those years, but I can say he
never pursued or dated any of them.

Judah graduated from high school, went on to Kansas City for
a Fire in the Night internship at the International House of Prayer,
and then went on to Sydney, Australia, for Hillsong's worship
school. While he was in Australia, John and I hired a children's
worker for the kid's ministry in the church we led at that time.
She was a former Youth With A Mission missionary and had spent
time in various nations of the world. When Judah returned from

Australia, he met her for the first time and says he immediately knew she, Bethany, was going to be his wife. A few weeks later, on Christmas Day, I had a dream. In the dream the Lord showed me Bethany was indeed Judah's wife and the years would reveal just how perfect they were for each other. On October 10, 2010 (10/10/10), John and I had the privilege to perform the wedding ceremony of our son and his bride. Bethany was our son's first date, his first kiss, his first everything. The purity of that relationship was exemplary.

Our two oldest daughters, Gabrielle and Aquila, have similarly taken Nazirite vows for periods of time in their lives. A time of separation and consecration unto the Lord, such as during a Nazirite vow, can help young adults be wholly given to the Lord and not distracted by relationships.

OUR STANDARDS

We have instructed our children in the courtship, or biblical dating, method. We have asked them not to engage in the modern process of dating. We are happy for our kids to hang out in groups with friends, or to go to coffee shops for conversations that build friendships or help them get to know someone. However, if a man pursues one of our daughters romantically with a more serious intention of dating, we have asked our daughters to have him request permission of John (or John and me) to court or biblically date our daughter. Our permission would only be granted if this is one John and I would consider someone our daughter could marry.

Scripture makes clear there is to be no sexual involvement outside of the covenant of marriage between one man and one woman. Fornication is sex outside of the covenant of marriage (1 Corinthians 6:9–10).

Besides the obvious, no physical intimacy until marriage, we have asked our children not to kiss until engagement. Well, the truth is, we asked them not to kiss until marriage, but our son found that too restrictive and asked about kissing upon engagement. I would still say the preferred is no kissing until marriage, but John and I are willing to work with our kids on that. Put simply, do not kiss before getting a ring, and do not take your clothing off until after the wedding. The question should never be, "How far can I go in physical touch and actions before it is too far before marriage?" The question should be, "How can I honour God and this person in my actions, maintaining the utmost purity?"

In the bat or bar barakah ceremonies we have held for our children at age thirteen, they sign a covenantal commitment, part of which states they commit to sexual purity, including abstinence until marriage. Mike Bickle suggests that young people who are beginning a dating relationship may find it beneficial to write down a list of things they will commit to in their relationship. The list might include activities to pursue (such as encouraging one another's spiritual vision, being actively involved in ministry, going to prayer meetings together, and reading the Word together) and activities to avoid (such as kissing before engagement, being in compromising situations, watching movies that stir up desires that cannot be righteously fulfilled, drinking alcohol together, being alone together in a home, etc.). In order to be accountable to uphold these standards, the couple should submit the written and signed commitments to parents or those they view as mentors.

Lastly, I advise all engaged couples to go through pre-marriage counseling because it identifies communication principles and forces the couple to think about future situations and to answer questions not obvious to them during their engagement.

SOUL TIES

I truly believe some of the sexual dysfunction presently experienced by adults may have spiritual roots in sexual sins in years past. First Corinthians 6 states that when we sin sexually it is not a sin outside the body, but *against* the body, since we become one with another person even though we are not covenanted together in spirit. Those involved in previous sexual and even emotional relationships with those who are not their spouses need to have soul ties broken with the other people.

I once was asked advice by a young man and woman in their twenties. They had known and liked each other since they were nine years old and had an on-again, off-again dating relationship for years. It was like they could not do without each other, but neither could they be together.

I asked if they were willing to have soul ties broken, to which they readily agreed. Separately, I took them through prayers of repentance for wrong ties to the other person, for physical acts done that crossed biblical lines, and for emotional attachments. Then we, by faith, asked the Lord to break the soul ties between the two of them, "sending back" parts of the other person's heart they had taken and asking for the part of their heart they had given up to "come back."

The results were immediate. The control and the ungodly ties were gone. Within just over a year each of those individuals had met and married the person they were destined by God to be with.

Girls should ask men whom they are considering committing to date if they have looked at pornography at all in the recent past (such as the last three months). With the tragic prevalence of addiction to pornography both in and outside the church, and its subsequent repercussions on relationships, it is important to see freedom in this area before any commitments are made to dating or marriage.

There is forgiveness and freedom for all, through the power of the cross, for previous relationships that crossed moral standards. However, healing, forgiveness, and freedom need to be sought out, applied, and then lived out. After Jesus forgave the woman caught in

MAY WE AS PARENTS HAVE THE WISDOM TO IMPART TO OUR CHILDREN GOD'S DESIGN FOR RELATIONSHIPS.

adultery, He also said, "Go and sin no more" (John 8:11). I feel grieved when I see young girls barely in their teens holding hands or kissing a young boy in the streets. Dating seems to be the norm in our culture at younger and younger ages. If they are kissing at age twelve, what will they be tempted to do at age eighteen? May we as parents have the wisdom to impart to our children God's design for relationships. Song of Solomon 2:7: "Do not stir up nor awaken love until it pleases."

LETTING GO

At age five, my mother told me life passes quickly and to cherish each stage. I didn't believe her since I thought going to grade one was torture and the days were so long. However, I have learned my mother was right! Time does pass so quickly, and I encourage all parents and mentors to cherish the time you have with the one in your care, at every stage of development. Don't try to rush through the baby stage, the time they are in diapers, the school years, or the time the child is dependent on you financially. Cherish it all.

The Genesis 2 admonishment to "leave and cleave" is not always easy for a parent. "Therefore a man shall leave his father and mother and be joined to his wife, and they shall become one flesh" (Genesis 2:24). When my oldest child, and only son, was leaving home at age seventeen for the ministry school 1,200 kilometres from our home, I went through a period of grieving. Truly, the time I had spent in mothering him at close range had passed all too quickly. Now I needed to release him and trust the Father in heaven to continue the work John and I had planted in his heart.

Judah's marriage was another stage of letting go. The realization I was no longer the most important woman in Judah's life was both a delight and a source of temporary, painful transition. Other than to God Himself, Judah's heart was rightly to be towards his wife before his parents.

These transitional stages—giving the car keys, sending off to college, walking down the aisle—they are both glorious and somewhat anguishing. There is a time when you, as a parent or as a mentor, need to step aside and allow the ones you love so much to soar in their God-given destiny. We never want to hold them back from being who God has called them to be, out of some need to keep them in our grasp. They always belonged to God. We were just given the privilege for a time to help fashion and form them for His purposes.

Although we never stop parenting, it takes on other forms as they grow. Friendships are formed. Grandparenting is another delight—to hold that precious bundle, knowing the generations are propagating. Another life is formed, forever destined to love and worship at the feet of Jesus. "A good man leaves an inheritance to his children's children" (Proverbs 13:22).

> **THERE IS A TIME WHEN YOU NEED TO STEP ASIDE AND ALLOW THE ONES YOU LOVE SO MUCH TO SOAR IN THEIR GOD-GIVEN DESTINY.**

We are gatekeepers. We are agents of blessing for our children, those we mentor, and for the generations to come. We help raise up ones with burning hearts on the earth. Joining with the generations as one voice of the bride longing for the Bridegroom, we say, along with the Spirit, "Come, Jesus, come" (Revelation 22:17).

NEXT GENERATION TESTIMONIAL

Judah Bootsma, our twenty-three-year-old son
STRATFORD, CANADA

When I was eleven years old, I was in a fling with a girl from church. I don't think we did more than hold hands for ten seconds. But, when you are young, it's a big deal. I eventually felt from the Lord (and my mom) that I needed to end whatever was happening. I remember having a download from God and seeing my heart like a pie. If I were eventually to go on dating girls and meandering through my teenage years doing the social norm, it would be like giving out my heart, pie piece by pie piece. Eventually, when I would want to settle down for marriage, what would I have left to give? (Not to say that there isn't redemption, forgiveness, and restoration through God.)

So with God's help, and a healthy dose of parental direction, I asked Him to keep my purity intact and committed to not go about dating until I was ready for marriage, or at least had a driver's license (that seemed a bit more doable at the time).

It wasn't always easy, and I often had to check my motives even with healthy friendships, so as to not get too involved under the "friendship" banner. But I made it, and it was so worth it! Giving my high school years to God brought such a base to live the rest of my life on, and a grounding as to who God was and who I was, rather than who other people would say I was. It's amazing how much you can learn from other people's mistakes, without having to get your feet wet trying them out yourself.

Even after I got my license, I was glad I had the maturity to wait until I knew who God had for me. I did some traveling and went to ministry schools at the International House of Prayer of Kansas City and then Hillsong in Australia. I thought I would surely meet someone in one of those places. Yet, there was never a peace about anyone. Suddenly, two days after returning home from Hillsong, I met the one. I know it doesn't always work this way, but I knew clearly from God that this is who He had for me. Bethany is the perfect complement for me and was way beyond what I had hoped, prayed, and thought about what I wanted in a wife.

I can't say for sure, but I don't think that the absolute peace and knowing would have come if I had lived life differently beforehand. What I can say, is that I am super glad I was able to come into a marriage with a whole heart to give. The fact that we waited has brought such ease, blessing, and joy into our lives and marriage.

I'm not saying this all as if it's a formula that will always work, or to brag about my story. But I am saying what is said in Proverbs

3:5–6, *"Trust in the* LORD *with all your heart, and lean not on your own understanding; in all your ways acknowledge Him, and He shall direct your paths."*

NOTES

1. Paul Strand, "Church Divorce Rate Way Lower than Anyone Thought," CBN News (2014): http://www.cbn.com/cbnnews/us/2014/June/Church-Divorce-Rate-Way-Lower-than-Anyone-Thought/
2. "What Is the Nazirite Vow?", accessed October 23, 2014, http://www.gotquestions.org/Nazirite-vow.html

APPENDIX: SUPERNATURAL CHILDBIRTH

Christ has redeemed us from the curse of the law, having become a curse for us.
GALATIANS 3:13

Having given birth to six children, I've learned a few things along the way. I'd like to preface this section with the fact that what I'm about to share I realize not all women experience. I have prayed for some pregnant women and had them come back to me and say, "My birth experience was just like you prayed!" I've also had others come back and say, "It was not like you prayed." Praying for someone else to have a supernatural birth experience is kind of like trying to pray your intimacy with the Lord into someone else. There may be an impartation of some sort, but the bottom line is we all have our own walk with God, our own journey of faith and miracles.

When I first felt regular contractions while pregnant with our first child, Judah, John and I got into his new car only to find it mysteriously had a flat tire! We then got into my car only to discover it wouldn't start—and I had never had that problem before! At two a.m. we called a dear friend, Gary Richards, to come take us to the hospital. We needn't have hurried because Judah came along thirty-six hours later weighing in at nine pounds, nine ounces.

I did not have any pain medication other than, at one point, being given an injection that helped me have a short sleep. I had a determination to do everything the natural way. At first sight of that bundle of joy I soon forgot the grueling labour and delivery. It was worth it all!

When Gabrielle came along two years later, I was more prepared but still felt every contraction, pushed through that "ring of fire," and stuck it out the natural way. I had a clear vision of Jesus in the delivery room when giving birth to Gabrielle. Jesus came close as if He were the one to catch her at delivery. In this vision I saw Him welcome her into the world with a tender heart of delight and love.

The birth of our third child, Aquila, changed the rest of my birthing experiences and catapulted me to a new level of faith for supernatural childbirths. I was nine months pregnant when John and I moved our family to Toronto and came on staff at Toronto Airport Christian Fellowship. Our first day on staff was May 23, 1995. On May 24 there was a conference at the church. Several of the speakers led in a prophetic prayer time at the end of the service. I was one who received a personal prophetic word. It was a greatly encouraging word about the anointing and destiny on my children and how the Lord would watch over them, "like they were in a safety deposit box, so the Lord will protect your children."

After the word, I went down under the power of the Spirit and lay near the front of the church soaking in the Lord's presence. As I lay there for perhaps an hour, I began to feel the tightening of contractions. Since the meeting was over, people were clearing the building, and John was talking to someone in the back of the large auditorium. Someone praying with me got on the microphone and said, "John Bootsma, please come to the front. Your wife is in labour." Along came John who helped me get up, and soon enough I found myself in the labour and delivery room of North York General Hospital. Hooked up to the belt-like contraction-measuring device, I could see the needles of the monitor moving rapidly at every abdominal muscle tightening. Yet I was completely oblivious to any sort of pain, as I was still basking in the warmth of the presence of God. It is like I was soaking while in labour! I could feel no pain, only the fact that my muscles were working as they are supposed to, such as if you go jogging. I shook and trembled under the power of His presence. Later, the labour-room doctor of twenty-five years stated, "That was the most unusual birth I have ever been in!" It was a supernatural delivery—I felt no pain. I was in complete peace, rest, and joy. We were delighted to welcome our daughter into our lives.

That experience proved to me it was possible to have a supernatural delivery. Thus, in giving birth to the next three children who came along, Phoebe, Zoe, and Glory Anna, I was determined to know how to access that same place of the weightiness of God's presence while in labour—and I did! In short, I learned to access His presence through His Word.

First of all, before labour, I would meditate on such scriptures as Galatians 3:13–14, "Christ has redeemed us from the curse of the law, having become a curse for us (for it is written, 'Cursed is everyone who hangs on a tree'), that the blessing of Abraham might come upon the Gentiles in Christ Jesus, that we might receive the promise of the Spirit through faith." Therein lie the keys—we are redeemed from the curse because of Jesus' sacrifice, and we access that redemption through faith and the power of the Holy Spirit.

In ancient Egypt, when the Hebrews were slaves in the land, Pharaoh became concerned about their proliferation, worried they could rise up in revolt. He devised a plan to murder the male Hebrew children, instructing the midwives to kill every male child upon birth but let the daughters live. The God-fearing midwives did not do as Pharaoh commanded and were called into his presence to give an explanation. Exodus 1:19 records, "And the midwives said to Pharaoh, 'Because the Hebrew women are not like the Egyptian women; for they are lively and give birth before the midwives come to them.'" In Hebrew the term *are lively (chayed)* means to have vigor of life, to bear quickly and easily. Accepting the fact that the Hebrew women gave birth differently from the Egyptian women, Pharaoh changed his plan of destruction to having the already-born male children cast into the river.

Perhaps the midwives were not telling the entire truth to Pharaoh, as the scripture makes clear they feared God and saved the male children. However, they also made the differentiation between the childbirth experiences of the Hebrew and Egyptian women. In other words, the women under the covenant of the Lord were different in their childbearing experiences from the women not under the covenantal blessing of the Lord. I also believe the same applies to today. We, as women of faith, are not to have the same experiences in childbirth as those who do not know Him. We are under blessing; we are in relationship; we have access to a supernatural life, including supernatural childbirth.

The same Hebrew word, *itstsabon*, translated pain over Eve in Genesis 3:16 (NASB), "'I will greatly multiply your pain in child-birth . . .'" was translated toil over Adam in Genesis 3:17 (NASB), "In toil you will eat of it [the ground]." I can accept the toil of la-bour. It is hard work. Your muscles are working hard. And that is a blessing! However, I learned to refuse to accept the "pain" part.

How a labouring woman views contractions is very important. If you fight against them, don't want them, or have adverse reac-tions to the God-designed working of your body, it takes peace away and brings a kind of counterproductive striving. I learned to see contractions as my friend, helping to bring the baby down to the birth canal and out into my arms. Willingly, even delightfully, accepting contractions as producing a desired effect helps us to em-brace them, desire them, and work with them.

When contractions would begin, I would meditate on a scrip-ture, repeating it over and over until I could feel myself getting lost in the glory and presence of God. Some of my favourite scriptures while in labor were Psalm 9:10, "And those who know Your name will put their trust in You; for You, LORD, have not forsaken those who seek You," and Psalm 29:11, "The LORD will give strength to His people; the LORD will bless His people with peace."

In chapter 5, we talked about how the written Word is to be a door through which we gain entry into the living Word—Jesus Himself. Jeanne Guyon, in her classic book *Experiencing the Depths of Jesus Christ*, teaches on beholding the Lord through scripture. After reading a short passage of scripture, she teaches, pause in gentle quietness, setting your mind on the Spirit. "Set your mind inwardly—on Christ," Jeanne exhorts the reader.

> The Lord is found *only* within your spirit, in the recesses of your being, in the Holy of Holies; this is where He dwells. The Lord once promised to come and make His home within you (John 14:23). He promised to there meet those who worship Him and who do His will. The Lord *will* meet with you in your spirit. It was St. Augustine who once said that he had lost much time in the beginning of his Christian experience by trying to find the Lord outwardly rather than by turning inwardly.[1]

Madame Guyon also speaks of how the physical senses can come into subjection to the spiritual senses—so we are not dictated to by how we feel in the natural, but what is going on in our spirits overcomes what is going on in the soul realm. That was how she was able to call her prison cell of ten years, in the Bastille in Paris, "heaven." She was not delusional. She was not in denial. She was a woman who learned to live out of her spirit. Misty Edwards' song "Garden" says it well: "I'm gonna live from the inside out."[2] Indeed, childbirth is an experience where we need to learn to live out of our spirit and not out of a natural realm of fear, pain, or anxiety. Of course, the practice of living out of our spirits in everyday life helps tremendously when we are in the labour room.

An excellent book I read just before giving birth to our fifth child gave words to my experiences. It is called *Supernatural Childbirth: Experiencing the Promises of God Concerning Conception and Delivery*, by Jackie Mize. I highly recommend it to all mothers-to-be.

John's role in the labour and delivery room was not as a bystander but an active participant. First Corinthians 7:4 states, "The wife does not have authority over her own body, but the husband does. And likewise the husband does not have authority over his own body, but the wife does." John took this scripture seriously and would use his authority over my body in prayer. He would speak to the cervix to speed up in thinning and dilating—and it would. He would speak to the muscles of my abdomen to contract without pain and help push the baby down the birth canal—and they would. Once, one of our children was in a breech position before birth; he spoke to the baby to turn, and that's what subsequently happened.

Transition is the stage of labour where the baby descends farther into the pelvis and the cervix completes dilation, readying the birth canal for the baby to crown and be born. It is often referred to as the most painful part of labour. In the birth of our daughter Zoe, I remember a time, right as transition was occurring, when I was losing my focus and my peace. Although we usually had Christian worship music playing in the delivery room, helping to create an atmosphere of the presence of God, we abandoned the music at that point, and John began to sing over me. He worshiped the Lord all the while hovering above me, massaging my head, and running his fingers through my hair. His worship over me catapulted me back into the realm of glory. I literally felt lifted up into the presence of the Lord. I needed John's strength at that point when I felt weak.

John was also such a blessing to massage my hands, arms, or feet with lotion. As mentioned in chapter 2, endorphins are released by touch and they produce a kind of natural analgesic.

ATMOSPHERE

The atmosphere of where we give birth is very important. Many today are choosing to have home births, and the usage of midwives is on the rise. I never did have a home birth, but had the next best thing in the birth of our last three children—a birthing centre within a hospital. It was a home-like atmosphere with Jacuzzis, rocking chairs, wallpaper on the walls, a private room, and amazing staff.

Wherever you choose to give birth, I recommend praying through the birthing room, welcoming the presence of God. If you are comfortable with it, have soaking worship music playing. Ensure that those you choose to have with you in the delivery room believe as you do regarding the birthing experience. For example, if you are believing for a supernatural childbirth, it wouldn't help to have a birthing coach who doesn't believe this is possible.

Aware of the fact that our family doctor worked on a rotational basis in the delivery room, I prayed for the right doctor and nurses to be our attendants at birth. During the birth of our daughter Zoe we were delighted to find out that not only was our assigned nurse a believer in Jesus, but also she attended our church. Amazingly, the doctor was also a strong believer who often attended our church. Because it is a large church, we didn't know her personally, but we were thrilled the Lord sent us a team of lovers of Jesus to be a part of our birthing experience.

A friend once recounted to me how she watched movies during early labour to distract and entertain herself. I was actually shocked when I heard that. I would never have dreamed of watching a movie while in labour. It was very important for me to focus. I would focus on the Lord, His presence, His nearness. I didn't even particularly like interacting with doctors or nurses in later stages of labour. I exercised getting lost in the presence of God, and anything that detracted me from His presence, I avoided.

I often compared childbirth to a kind of sporting event, like an athlete would train for the Olympics—training our spirit to walk in faith, our mind to be in peace, and our body to be subject to the higher realm of the presence of God. I spent time in prayer while pregnant, praying for a glorious delivery. When it comes time to give birth we are ready—in our spirit, mind, will, emotions, and in our body.

The last four of my six childbirth experiences were pain free, glorious, and filled with the presence of God. I discovered having a supernatural delivery—one filled with the presence of God—is attainable. We simply need to access it. I believe there are many things that were accomplished for us by the shed blood of Jesus on the cross that we are not accessing yet. He died for us to have abundant life (John 10:10). That means not only did He die for us to receive forgiveness of our sins and life eternal, He also died for us to extravagantly enjoy life. That includes enjoying the childbirth experience. With God, indeed, all things are possible.

But Jesus looked at them and said to them, "With men this is impossible, but with God all things are possible."
MATTHEW 19:26

NOTES

1. Jeanne Guyon, *Experiencing the Depths of Jesus Christ*, ed. Gene Edwards (Jacksonville: SeedSowers Publishing, 1975), 11.
2. Misty Edwards, "Garden," *Relentless*. Kansas City, MO: Forerunner Music, 2007.

DID YOU ENJOY
RAISING BURNING HEARTS?

Recommend the eBook to a friend.
Available for Kindle, Nook, and iBooks.

ihopkc.org/raisingburninghearts

ANOTHER RECOMMENDED BOOK
FROM PATRICIA BOOTSMA
Convergence: Heaven's Destiny Becoming Your Reality

In this book you will walk beside Patricia on her journey of discovery, and in doing so you will gain keys to unlock the doors of your destiny. You will discover how to recognize the depths of God's Father-love toward you, how to respond to it, and how to allow it to change your life; find the keys to healing your heart so you are capable of receiving prophetic fulfillment; live the prophetic lifestyle daily; successfully make prophetic decrees that change your life and the lives of others; and much more.

Isn't it time you experience the convergence of heaven's desire for your life—both in the here and now and in the eternal realm to come?

Patricia's book Convergence: Heaven's Destiny Becoming Your Reality *is a must-read for any hungry student of the prophetic. It is one of those books that you will probably want to buy two of—one for your own library and another to lend to others.* Convergence: Heaven's Destiny Becoming Your Reality, *with its solid, foundational teachings, can also be used in Bible studies and training classes as a lesson topic guide. I highly recommend this book!*

—Patricia King, XP Ministries

For booking engagements
and additional resources
visit **patriciabootsma.com**

INTERNATIONAL HOUSE *of* PRAYER

24/7 LIVE WORSHIP AND PRAYER
ihopkc.org/prayerroom

Since September 19, 1999, we have continued in night-and-day prayer with worship as the foundation of our ministry to win the lost, heal the sick, and make disciples, as we labor alongside the larger Body of Christ to see the Great Commission fulfilled, and to function as forerunners who prepare the way for the return of Jesus.

By the grace of God, we are committed to combining 24/7 prayers for justice with 24/7 works of justice until the Lord returns. We believe we are better equipped to reach out to others when our lives are rooted in prayer that focuses on intimacy with God and intercession for breakthrough of the fullness of God's power and purpose for this generation.

International House of Prayer Missions Base, 3535 E. Red Bridge Road, Kansas City, MO 64137
(816) 763-0200 | info@ihopkc.org

INTERNATIONAL
HOUSE *of* PRAYER
UNIVERSITY

MINISTRY • MUSIC • MEDIA • MISSIONS

....

ENCOUNTER GOD. DO HIS WORKS. CHANGE THE WORLD.
ihopkc.org/ihopu

....

International House of Prayer University (IHOPU) is a full-time Bible school which exists to equip this generation in the Word and in the power of the Holy Spirit for the bold proclamation of the Lord Jesus and His return.

As part of the International House of Prayer, our Bible school is built around the centrality of the Word and 24/7 prayer with worship, equipping students in the Word and the power of the Spirit for the bold proclamation of the Lord Jesus and His kingdom. Training at IHOPU forms not only minds but also lifestyle and character, to sustain students for a life of obedience, humility, and anointed service in the kingdom. Our curriculum combines in-depth biblical training with discipleship, practical service, outreach, and works of compassion.

IHOPU is for students who long to encounter Jesus. With schools of ministry, music, media, and missions, our one- to four-year certificate and diploma programs prepare students to engage in the Great Commission and obey Jesus' commandments to love God and people.

> "What Bible School has 'prayer' on its curriculum? The most important thing a man can study is the prayer part of the Book. But where is this taught?
>
> Let us strip off the last bandage and declare that many of our presidents and teachers do not pray, shed no tears, know no travail. Can they teach what they do not know?"
>
> –Leonard Ravenhill, *Why Revival Tarries*

International House of Prayer University, 12901 S. US Highway 71, Grandview, MO 64030
(816) 763-0243 | info@ihopu.org

International House *of* Prayer

INTERNSHIPS

INTRO TO IHOPKC • FIRE IN THE NIGHT • ONE THING INTERNSHIP
SIMEON COMPANY • HOPE CITY INTERNSHIP

ihopkc.org/internships

Internships exist to see people equipped with the Word of God, ministering in the power of the Holy Spirit, engaged in intercession, and committed to outreach and service.

Our five internships are three to six months long and accommodate all seasons of life. The purpose of the internships is to further prepare individuals of all ages as intercessors, worshipers, messengers, singers, and musicians for the work of the kingdom. While each internship has a distinctive age limit, length, and schedule, they all share the same central training components: corporate prayer and worship meetings, classroom instruction, practical ministry experience, outreach, and relationship-building.

Biblical teaching in all of the internships focuses on intimacy with Jesus, ministry in the power of the Holy Spirit, the forerunner ministry, evangelizing the lost, justice, and outreach. Interns also receive practical, hands-on training in the prophetic and healing ministries.

Upon successful completion of a six-month internship or two three-month tracks, some will stay and apply to join IHOPKC staff.

Our IHOPKC Leadership Team

Our leadership team of over a hundred and fifty men and women, with diversity of experience, background, and training, represents twenty countries and thirty denominations and oversees eighty-five departments on our missions base. With a breadth of experience in pastoral ministry, missions work, education, and the marketplace, this team's training in various disciplines includes over forty master's degrees and ten doctorates.

International House of Prayer Missions Base, 3535 E. Red Bridge Road, Kansas City, MO 64137
(816) 763-0200 | internships@ihopkc.org